The Temple Religious School
UNIVERSITY CIRCLE AT SILVER PARK
CLEVELAND, OHIO 44106

TALES
of
the PROPHET SAMUEL

*

*

TALES
of
the PROPHET SAMUEL

retold for Jewish youth

by Rabbi Charles Wengrov

Illustrated by Aharon Shevo

*

SHULSINGER BROTHERS

NEW YORK

Copyright 1969 by Shulsinger Brothers, Inc.

Set in Linotype Times Roman 14 point (with
Century Schoolbook, Bulmer, and Foundry Times Roman).
Composed and printed at the Press of Shulsinger Brothers
21 East 4th Street / New York, NY 10003

*All rights reserved. No part of this book may be reproduced
in any form without permission in writing from the publisher,
except by a reviewer, who may quote brief passages and
reproduce not more than one illustration in a review
to be printed in a magazine or newspaper.*

Manufactured in the United States of America

contents

1	Off to Shiloh	7
2	"Come Along with Us"	13
3	Hannah Goes to Pray	18
4	The Child is Born	28
5	The Early, Happy Years	33
6	Growing Up in Shiloh	41
7	Sons of Evil	53
8	The Voice from the Ark	64
9	War with the Philistines	72
10	Of Mice and a Plague	91
11	The Ark Returns	101
12	Samuel Takes Charge	115

1

OFF TO SHILOH

NEVER HAD THE SUN shone so beautifully, thought Elkanah, as he watched its rays spread above the hills of Samaria, painting the sky with color and light. But with so much to do, he had no time to stand and look. This was the day to start the journey to Shiloh. His wife Ḥannah was already at work inside the house, preparing the food they would need in the days ahead.

In another part of the house the children were getting up, some crying, some chattering and laughing. They were the sons of his second wife, Peninnah (for in those early times in the Land of Israel it was quite usual for a man to live with more than one wife). In a moment Peninnah rose, to wash and dress her young ones.

As Elkanah passed by the house on his way to the barn, through the open window he heard Peninnah's voice, high and laughing with scorn: "Well, Ḥannah — why do you not wash *your* children and get them dressed?" Elkanah clenched his fists in anger. He did not have to be in the house to know that his beloved Ḥannah would now turn white, and keep silent, trying to hold back her tears. It was about the same every morning, the year 'round. While all were yet in their beds, as the children began to stir and make noise, Peninnah would rise and ask in her mocking, laughing voice, "Well, Hannah, will you not get up from your sleep to get *your* children washed? Come, get them dressed and give them breakfast, so that they can go to school and learn Torah."

What could Hannah ever say? In all the years of her marriage no children had been born to her. Elkanah did not mind. He loved Hannah dearly, and she made him happy. And he had not wanted any second wife either. But when ten years of their life together had gone by and she still had no children, the sweet and gentle Hannah began to insist, "You must take another wife, Elkanah. A man needs children — stalwart sons to take their place by his side, lovely daughters to make him proud."

Again and again Elkanah said no. But in her love for him, Hannah kept insisting; and at last he gave in. He took Peninnah for a second wife. And how very sorry he now was. True, Peninnah bore him ten fine, healthy boys. But she was always jealous that Elkanah loved Hannah more than her, and whenever she could she made Hannah suffer. Once she taunted Hannah, "Do you think Elkanah will always love you because you are beautiful? You will grow old; your beauty will vanish. Then he will see that you are nothing but a barren tree that bears no fruit. And he will love me for the children I have given him."

Ḥannah had wept so bitterly then. Days went by before Elkanah could stop her tears and bring a smile to her face.

As he went on to the barn, Elkanah kept thinking. If only there were some way he could make Peninnah be still. But there was nothing he could do. She was the mother of his children. He could neither punish her nor drive her out of his home. And if he spoke to her, she simply did not listen. Well, thought Elkanah, now that they were going to Shiloh for the *ḥag,* for the Festival, perhaps they would forget their troubles for a while and just be happy.

After he fed the animals in the barn, he went to make the wagon ready for the trip. A wheel had to be mended, and Elkanah worked carefully. The wagon was very large; yet he knew that when they set out there would be not an inch of space to spare.

The sun was high in the sky by the time he had the wagon ready. As he went to harness the horses, his kinsmen and relatives began to arrive from their neighboring farms. Ḥannah and Peninnah came out with smiles of greeting, and the children came bouncing after them with bubbling laughter and whoops of joy. It was months since their kinsmen had last visited them.

The first to go into the wagon was not a person at all, but a ram, a fine animal with two horns growing from its head. Next they put in a lamb. Obeying the laws of the Torah, Elkanah would bring the two to Shiloh as sacrifices to the Almighty, and then the animals would provide enough food for them all for several days. Then his family took their places, together with their relatives and kinsmen. When the last child had been carried up and all were settled comfortably, Elkanah took up the reins, and the horses set off. They were away at last.

As they ambled along, Elkanah looked at his village of Ramah, marked by the white walls of its low houses, and he thought again how lovely it was. Set in a wild region, the village lay among green woods, near streams whose waters always ran swiftly. No farmer in Ramah would ever go thirsty or watch his fields go dry for lack of water. Snugly the village nestled between two hills high enough to serve as watching posts for sentries in time of danger (and for this reason it was often called *Ramathayim Tzofim*, "the two hills of the watchers").

Suddenly Elkanah heard an outburst of children's laughter behind him in the wagon, and he turned around to see why. Days before, as they were making ready for the trip, the boys had secretly prepared garlands of flowers and green olives, strung together on strong threads. These the children now placed around the necks of the ram and the lamb, and the animals looked funny indeed. Elkanah laughed too, as he saw Hannah and Peninnah smiling, all their enmity and bitterness now forgotten.

His heart felt lighter. Perhaps they would really have a good holiday in Shiloh. Even the horses' hoofs

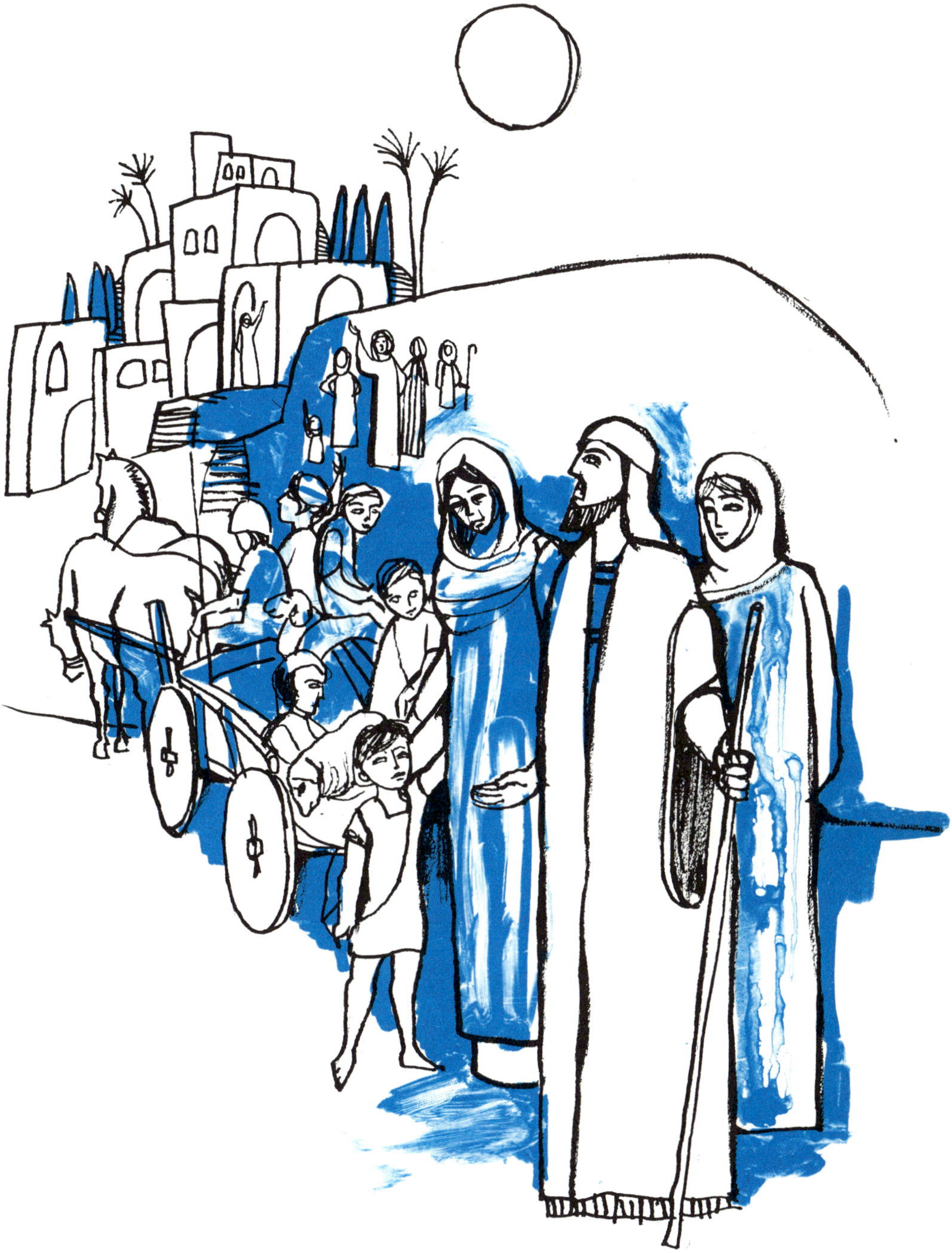

seemed to strike the road now in a happy beat as they gathered speed.

But the children were not finished. As they left their village behind them, they took out more garlands and strings of flowers, olives, and fruits. When they strung these across the sides of the wagon, everything began to look festive and gay. Soon they were singing merrily, while the horses cantered on.

2

"COME ALONG WITH US"

It was about twelve miles from Ramah to Shiloh. Had Elkanah taken the wagon in a straight route, they would have arrived in a few hours. But as he drove the horses, the course they took was anything but straight. To the right and left they turned following a most bewildering zigzag path. For Elkanah had one purpose in mind: to take the wagon through towns and villages.

Soon after Ramah disappeared from their view, the wagon entered the next town. Elkanah slowed the horses to a walk, and in no time at all children gathered to follow. Then adults began watching and following too. For it was strange indeed to see a wagon filled with people and two animals and decorated with garlands of flowers and fruits, while the children in the wagon sang,

> *We're happy to know*
> *that away we go*
> *to see the House of the Lord.*

Elkanah stopped the wagon altogether, and the townspeople gathered around. "Where are you going?"

they asked. And Elkanah began to explain: "My friends, when our forefathers left Egypt and travelled through the wilderness to reach this Promised Land of ours, their great leader Moses taught them (as the Almighty taught him) to build a *mishkan,* a Tabernacle, as a holy House of God." The people gathered closer to listen. They had heard about Moses and their forefathers in the wilderness; but living alone in their little village, they had never had a chance to learn very much. In fact, from the people of the nations around them, many learned to keep idols in their homes, to worship and pray to them — and they did not know they were doing anything wrong. Now, at last, someone stood before them to tell them about the early years of their people and about Moses, the first and greatest leader of the Hebrews.

Elkanah spoke on, describing the *mishkan* that the Hebrews had built in the wilderness. Then his voice rang out: "Do you know where that *mishkan* is today? It stands in Shiloh. And there my family and my kinsmen and I are going — because tomorrow evening a Hebrew festival begins. Here, let me read to you what our Torah commands us."

As he took out a great parchment scroll, his listeners stirred and looked up in open-mouthed wonder. They had heard of the Torah, the great Book that the Almighty had told Moses to write; but hardly had they ever seen one. Elkanah now opened it and read, "Three times in the year shall all your menfolk appear before the Lord your God in the place that He will choose: on the Festival of *Matzot* (Passover), on the Festival of *Shavuot,* and on the Festival of *Sukkot.*"

For a moment Elkanah was silent. Then he continued: "The place He has chosen, the place where His presence dwells, is the *mishkan* in Shiloh. I ask you: Go to Shiloh now, as my family and I are going; and let us spend the Festival there together, as the Torah commands. There you will learn more of this precious Torah. You will learn how to serve the true God who created heaven and earth."

"We will go! We will go!" came a great shout from the townspeople. To their homes they went to pack and make ready. And Elkanah set the wagon rolling again on its turning, meandering journey through hills and valleys.

Tired of sitting, Elkanah's oldest son got up to stand beside him and watch the road. "Father," he said after a while, "when we went to Shiloh last year, we did not go this way at all. Why are we taking a different route this time?"

"Did you hear what I told the people in that town?" asked Elkanah. His son nodded. "Last year," Elkanah continued, "when we went by a different route, we rode through other towns, and I told the people there the same thing. They went to Shiloh, and they heard Eli the *kohen gadol* (the high priest) teaching the Torah. They know that they should go now to Shiloh again. They do not need me to tell them. The time before that we went through still other towns; but you were much too young then, and you do not remember. Every time we go, we will take a different route, so that I can tell more and more people to come with us. Why, years ago — before you were born — hardly any families would turn up at Shiloh for a Festival. All over the land our people are busy with their farms and their cattle, and they do not learn or remember what the Torah teaches. But if I stop at a town and talk to the people, five or ten families come along, and they start going to Shiloh. And for every Festival afterward, more and more families go along with them. You will see: When Eli the *kohen gadol* comes out to teach the Torah, there will be a good-sized crowd listening to him."

It was late at night when they reached the next town. Under the clear silver moon and the diamond-bright stars the town slept; not a soul was stirring. Elkanah stopped the wagon by the side of the road, and in the mild and pleasant air his family spread blankets in an open field. Soon they too were fast asleep.

Hardly had the day begun when people began to notice the wagon by the road, so gaily decorated with flowers and fruits. Like the inhabitants of the other town, they also gathered about in great curiosity, eager to find out who were riding in it, and why.

They did not have to wait long. Soon Elkanah was

up in the wagon, talking long and earnestly, showing them his Torah and reading from it. And the people were glad he had come to them. Two hours later, when Elkanah started up his horses and the wagon wheels began to roll, five families of the town rode along behind him.

As he drove on, Elkanah felt gladness spread through his heart. It would not be long, he knew, before another five households in Israel would smash their idols of wood and stone, having learned to worship the one true Creator and Ruler of the world.

3

HANNAH GOES TO PRAY

On a rounded rocky hill stood the little town of Shiloh. East, north, and west of it lay deep valleys; but further out rose steeper hills, to frame the little town in a picturesque, dream-like setting.

On the day before the Festival, families kept coming and coming — far more then Elkanah had ever expected — and he was pleased. For many who had been there before brought along friends and neighbors this time.

Elkanah found an open field where he could pitch his tent. There his family settled down to eat the evening meal and sleep the night. In the morning Hannah and he took the ram to the *mishkan,* so that a son of Eli the *kohen gadol* might offer it as a sacrifice to the Almighty. Soon after, meat was cooking over an open fire in a shallow pit. In a little while it would be ready for their festive meal.

The meat was still quite hot when Elkanah began cutting off pieces for everyone. To each he gave a fair

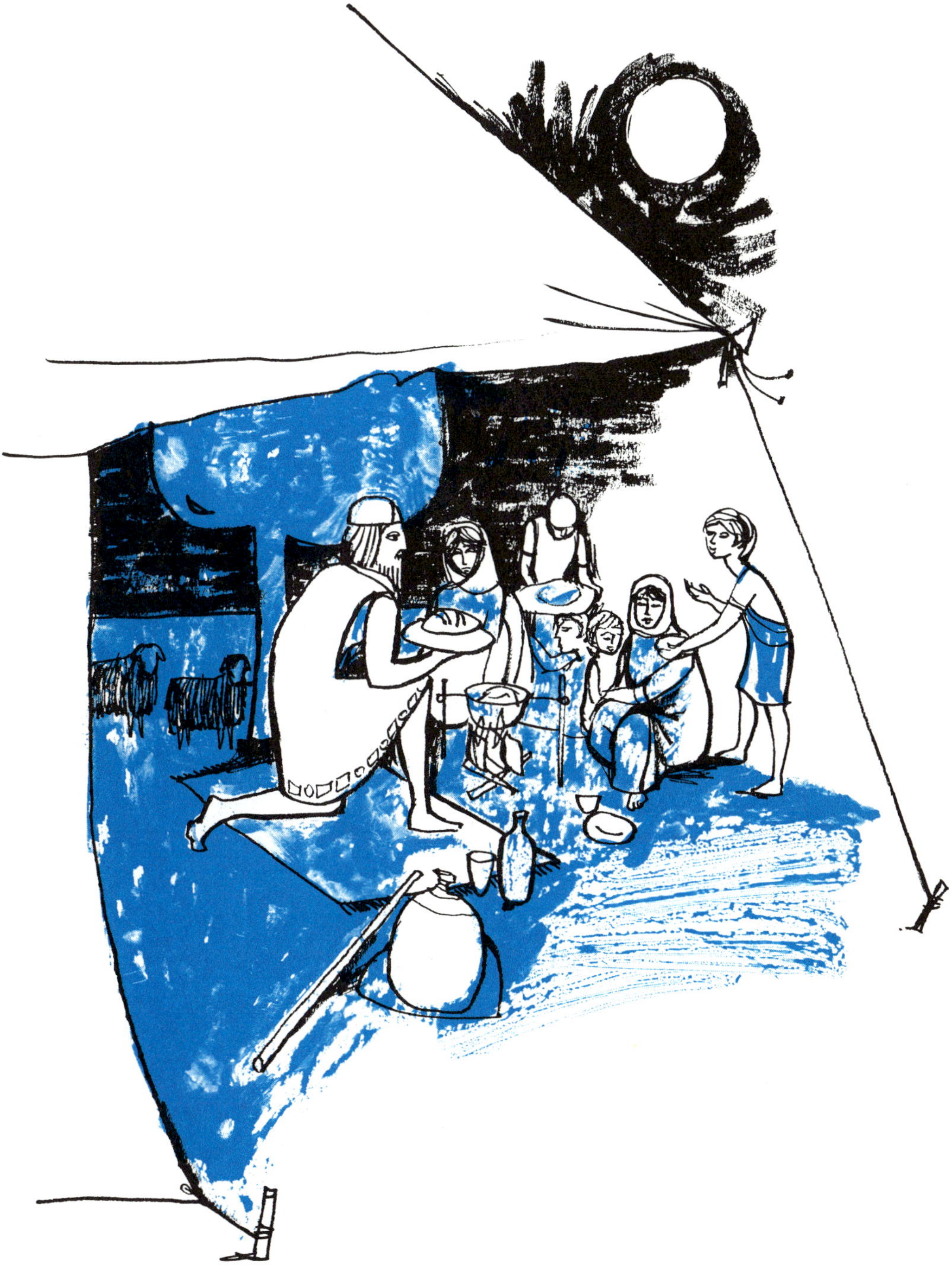

share, as they sat about on the meadow grass. Then he found an especially choice piece of meat, tastier and better-cooked than all the rest. Without a moment's thought he gave it to Ḥannah, the one he loved the best. Peninnah watched, and jealousy filled her heart again; and her eyes became cruel. Her whisper was low, so that Ḥannah alone could hear:

"You think you are the lucky one because Elkanah loves you. But Heaven has made *me* the lucky one, not you. If you are so gentle and good, why has the Almighty let you have not one child? Well, you will see. The years will go by, and Elkanah will love me, not you, for the children I have given him."

And tears came once again to Ḥannah's eyes. How she longed for a child, to hold it and fondle it and care for it, to watch it grow bigger until it could walk and run and play. Why was it her fate to be childless?

The choice piece of meat lay before her untasted, until Elkanah noticed it, and all happiness left him too. Why did it have to happen again? he wondered. Every time at Shiloh he gave Ḥannah the best of the food because he loved her dearly. And every time Peninnah taunted her and hurt her until tears swam in her eyes and she could not touch her food.

Elkanah drew close to her. "Ḥannah," he murmured, "why are you weeping? Why do you not eat? Your heart should not be heavy with grief. This is a Festival, a time to rejoice. Come, no more tears now.

Be happy with us. What does it matter if Peninnah has ten children? Am I not better to you than ten sons?" Through her tears Ḥannah smiled at him and took up her food.

But as she ate an idea took hold of her. She remembered how she had gone with Elkanah in the morning to the *mishkan,* to bring the ram for sacrifice. Before they gave the animal to one of Eli's two sons, Elkanah had bowed down in the courtyard and prayed to the Almighty. He did the same at every Festival in Shiloh. This morning, though, she had grown curious. "Why do you bow down and pray as soon as we come here?" she asked him. Gravely he replied, "Because prayer is more beloved to the Almighty than all the offerings and sacrifices. When we pray we speak our hearts to the Almighty; and sometimes we can hear His answer." But she was still puzzled. "You pray at home," she asked him. "Why must you say more words here?"

As she ate her meat now, she remembered clearly his answer: "This is the House of the Lord. One thought of honest prayer here can do more for you than hundreds of words at home. Here you can feel His holiness."

It was early afternoon when the meal ended. Now all lay resting, and Elkanah dozed.

Silently Ḥannah rose and made her way to the courtyard of the *mishkan.* There was much she wanted to say to the Almighty; and she had her husband's word that here was the best place in all the world to speak before Him.

"Almighty Lord," she began in a whisper. Afraid that Peninnah might have secretly followed her to watch from some nearby hiding place, she wanted to make sure no human being could hear a word. She did not want to be taunted and mocked any more. "Almighty Lord, I look about me at the great many people who have come up to Shiloh. And I see fathers and mothers happy with the children that were born to them. O Lord, You are the Creator of heaven and earth, and the host of living beings that fill them. Can You then not give me one little boy?"

She had not meant to weep, but the tears came of themselves, out of the years of bitterness that lay stored in her heart. For a long while she stood there, two streams of tears running down her cheeks, her shoulders shaking with her sobs. And then, all at once, she knew what else she had to say; the words seemed to come of themselves, and her heart agreed to them: "O Lord of the hosts (of heaven and earth), if only You will see the suffering of Your poor servant here; if only You will remember me and not forget Your servant; O, if only You will give Your servant a living son — I will give him back to You. I will give him to the Lord, that he may serve You all the days of his life; and never will the fear of any man rule his thoughts. Lord, take pity on me, for I cannot bear my sorrow any longer. Grant me a wise son, who will be understanding and devout, that he may serve You well."

On and on the words came, but all in a whisper. Wrapped completely in her prayer, she neither saw nor heard anything about her. She did not realize that there in front, on his chair by the doorpost at the entrance to the *mishkan* itself, sat Eli the *kohen gadol* (high priest), in charge of this House of the Lord. Ever since she had come into the courtyard he sat watching her. Hearing not a word of hers, he saw only a woman standing, sometimes swaying a bit back and forth, her lips moving and the tears falling from her eyes. She looked wretched and miserable to Eli; he could not understand why she was there. She could certainly not be praying, he thought: When people prayed, they spoke up. Then he remembered that it was just after the festive midday meal. She must have taken too much wine, he decided.

"Woman!" Eli called out. Startled, she looked up, seeing him for the first time. "How long will you go on drinking too much?" he cried. "And why do you come here after all the wine? Go home and hide your shame; and get your wine out of your system."

"O no, my lord," Ḥannah exclaimed. "I am but a woman of anguished spirit, nothing more. No wine or strong drink have I taken. I have only come to pour out my soul in prayer before the Lord. Do not think your servant a wicked woman who fills herself with wine, to her shame. There was so much I had to say to our Ruler in heaven, so much vexation in me, that I had to speak before Him."

Eli was truly sorry for his harsh words; this poor woman had not deserved them. He could hear in her voice that she told the truth. "Forgive me that I have shamed you," he begged her. "Go now in peace, and may the God of Israel grant you what you have asked of Him."

Ḥannah bowed low. "May your servant find grace and favor in your eyes, that you may ask Heaven's mercy for me."

"Never fear," said Eli. "There are times when I see some of the things that go on in the Almighty's heavenly world. And now I see that your prayer has reached Him, and He will answer you well. Imagine a poor man, a beggar, who comes to a great banquet that a king has made for all his royal servants. The beggar stands at the door of the banquet hall and pleads, *Give me a piece of bread . . . a piece of bread*; but so busy are the servants eating and drinking and enjoying themselves, that they have no time to spare for him. Desperately hungry, the poor man pushes his way through the hall until he reaches the king himself. *Your Majesty*, says he, *from this whole great banquet that you have made, would it be so hard for you to give me a piece of bread?*"

Ḥannah looked at the *kohen gadol* in amazement. That was exactly the kind of thing she had said to the

Almighty. How did he know? But before she could say a word, Eli spoke on:

"Now, the king has time to listen and to help the hungry man. Even so have you reached the Almighty Himself with your words and your tears; and He will answer. You shall have a son who will learn the Torah well!"

Ḥannah was halfway back to her tent when a greater wonder made her stop. For suddenly she thought: How did Eli ever know it was a son she wanted? That she had not told him. She had only said she came to pray because she was sorely troubled.

It came to Ḥannah that Eli must really be something of a prophet or a seer, who, as he said, sometimes learned of matters in Heaven that ordinary people could not know. And he had clearly told her she *would* have a son! He must have learned that from Heaven too!

Gone was her face of suffering and sorrow as she returned to her tent. In its place was a shining look of simple joy. From then on, no matter what Peninnah said to her, she remained cheerful. She ate well, and there was always a smile on her face. And Elkanah felt happy with her.

As for Eli the *kohen gadol,* he often thought about Ḥannah. There was one thing he had not told her: About a month before she came, he had heard a strange distant voice, a heavenly echo, which foretold that soon someone named Samuel would be born, who would become

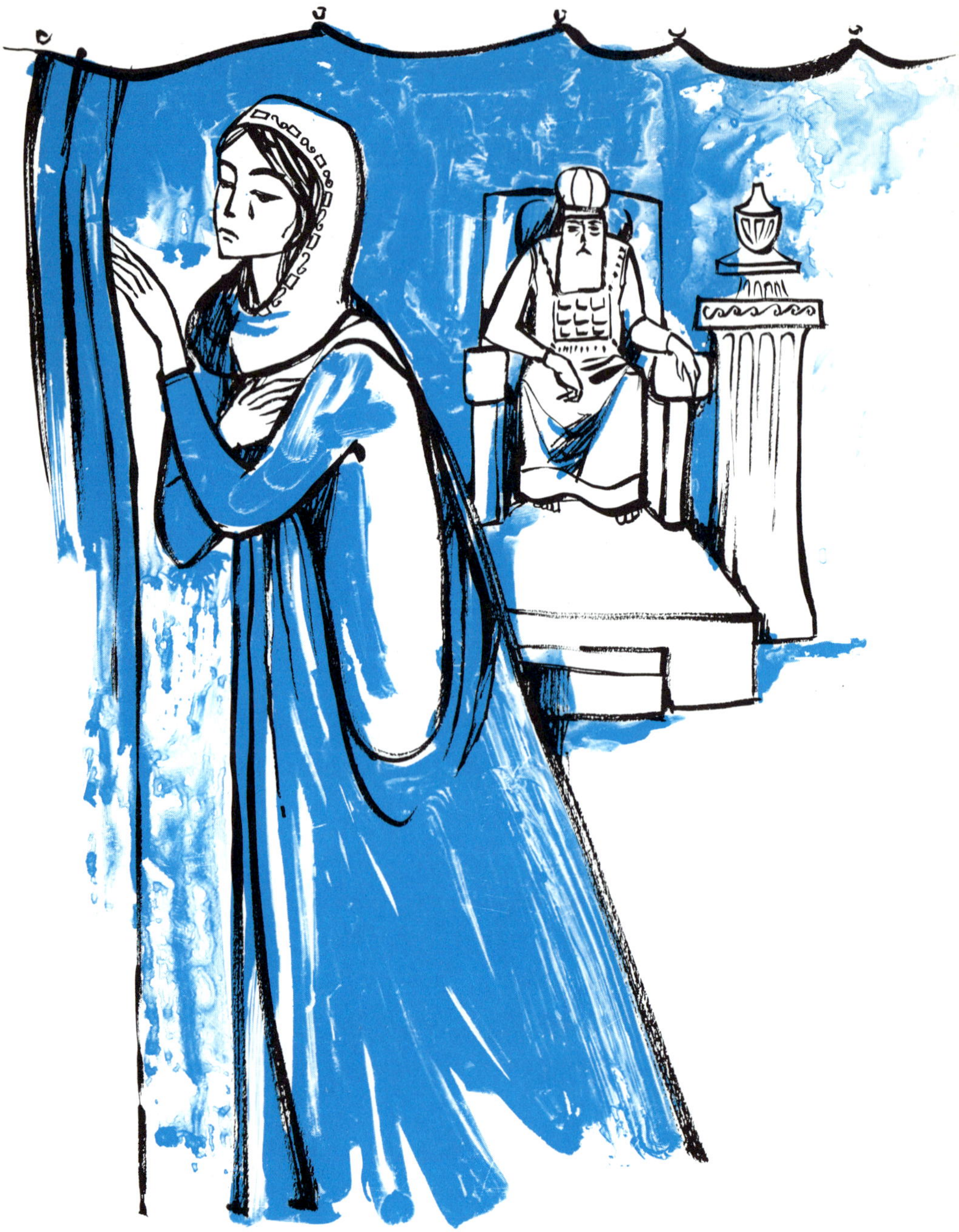

a great, wise prophet to his people. The more Eli thought about it, the more certain he became: This Samuel would be the child that Ḥannah was going to have. Somehow, he knew it in his heart.

4

THE CHILD IS BORN

Back in Ramah, Ḥannah lived in peaceful happiness as the months went by. In time Eli's prophetic words came true, and she gave birth to a fine handsome boy. And in all Ramah no father knew greater joy than Elkanah. For an hour at a time or more he could stand by the bedside watching the baby sleeping near its mother.

"What shall we name him?" he asked her.

"I would like to call him *Sh'muel*," she answered, "from the words *sha-ul me-el*, 'asked from God.' You see, he came only because I asked the Almighty for him in my prayers." So his name became *Sh'muel*, which in English is Samuel. Little did Ḥannah suspect that the unseen Ruler of the world had put it into her mind to give the child this name — because he was to be the great prophet that the heavenly echo had promised.

Nor did Ḥannah know that in other parts of Israel other children were being named Samuel. For when Eli the *kohen gadol* heard the strange voice from heaven, there were others with the power of a prophet or seer who heard it also. As they told of it, the word spread through their towns and villages: A child named Samuel would be born who would grow up to be a very great prophet. So one mother after another gave her infant boy this name, hoping *he* would become this wonderful, outstanding leader of his people. And when these mothers and their friends came together, they would always look carefully at the little children, to see if any looked bright and intelligent. Then each would eagerly ask the other, "Well, how is *your* Samuel? Does he show any signs that he will be the one? Did he begin talking at an early age? Did he begin walking at an early age?" Many a mother thought she saw something especially wonderful or clever in her little boy, and she would eagerly boast of it to friends and neighbors. And if a little lad named Samuel really said something bright or did something extraordinary — even if he only learned a hard word or did a somersault — the news spread like wildfire in his neighborhood: "Did you hear what that child said?" people told one another. "Did you hear what that child did? He will surely grow up to be the prophet that we are all expecting . . ."

Yet after a while, in one town after another, people realized that there was nothing remarkable about any of these children. They were quite normal and ordinary, nothing more.

Sadly the people shook their heads: "No, we have

not yet seen this wonderful future prophet Samuel. It may be that he has not been born yet."

Hannah, however, heard nothing of all this in her lovely, peaceful village of Ramah. Quietly, calmly she took care of her child, and watched him grow day after day. As she cuddled him, sang to him, and fed him, she sometimes remembered what Peninnah had called her: a barren tree that could bear no fruit. Now she felt like a tree that has grown a fine ripe fruit; in her heart she was content.

And knowing nothing of a heavenly echo, Hannah did not watch her child closely or try to compare him with other children. Whatever he was, she loved him dearly and was glad to have him. It was her neighbors and friends, who often came to visit on a pleasant afternoon, who noticed how different this baby was. "Look at him," they remarked. "His eyes seem to study everything and watch everything. We have never seen a child look so wise and understanding."

"My prayers must have made him like that," said Hannah, laughing.

"Do you mean you prayed that he should be wise and all-knowing?" asked a neighbor.

"Oh yes," replied the happy mother; "and religious too."

"But why?" asked the neighbor. "Why did you not pray that your child should be handsome and wealthy? That is what every woman always prays for."

"But do you not see?" asked Ḥannah. "I took a vow that if the Almighty gave me a child, I would give him to the Lord, to serve his Maker all the days of his life. When someone has to devote his life to the Almighty, what good is it to him to be handsome and rich? However, the more wisdom, understanding and devotion he has, the better he can serve his Creator.

"I will tell you," Ḥannah continued. "When I prayed for a son so that I could give him to the Almighty, I thought of someone who wants to make a crown for a king. Any rare jewel or precious gem he has, he should use for the crown, to make it more splendid and valuable. For after all, the crown will be placed on the king's head. So did I ask that if my son is to spend his life serving the Almighty, let him have a fine character, a good heart, and a good mind."

Her neighbors looked at Ḥannah in wonder. They thought how well and truly Elkanah and Ḥannah deserved such a good child. Not only was Ḥannah good and gentle; Elkanah worked hard at every Festival to bring new Hebrew families to Shiloh. Heaven was now rewarding them.

Months passed; and once more it was two days before a Festival. Again Elkanah went to the barn, to the horses and the wagon. Peninnah worked busily to make her ten sons ready for the journey. But Ḥannah sat in her corner as always, gently rocking her child by the sunlit window.

When Elkanah was ready, he went into the house. "Ḥannah," said he, "our kinsmen will soon be here, and we will set out for Shiloh. Will you not take little Samuel and come with us?"

Ḥannah smiled. "Forgive me, dear husband, if the child and I do not go with you. He is a frail thing, and not strong. I fear for his health if we should take him to Shiloh. Let us two stay here at home, until he grows old enough to get along without my care. Then I will bring him to the holy House at Shiloh, to stand in the presence of the Lord. Then I will keep my vow and let him remain there for the rest of his life."

Elkanah kissed her forehead. "Do what seems best to you," he said. "Stay home until he will be a big boy. After all, Eli gave you the Almighty's promise that you would have a son who would live. If we take him to Shiloh, he can take sick on the way and die. We must make sure the Lord's promise is fulfilled. You stay and take care of him." With another kiss for the child, he was off.

5

THE EARLY, HAPPY YEARS

The next few years seemed to Ḥannah like a long sweet dream, as she watched her son growing. Not since she had been a child herself at her mother's knee had she felt such pure happiness. Little Samuel was a real boy. He learned to walk and run and play. Then he learned to talk and to understand the words of others. And always there came into his eyes the look of great wisdom that the neighbors had noticed when he was still an infant . . . as though he knew and understood everything in people's hearts . . . as though he could see and hear things far away.

As he grew older, Ḥannah told him about the *mishkan* at Shiloh, the holy House of the Almighty. She told Samuel how she had prayed for him there, because no child had ever been born to her. And she told him of her oath — how she had solemnly promised the Almighty that if she would have a boy she would bring him to that holy House and leave him there — and there the boy would grow up to be a true servant of the Ruler of the world.

At other times Samuel would laugh and romp and giggle. But whenever his mother spoke of this, the wondrous look of wisdom came back to his face. He listened quietly to every word, and nodded his little head. And as his mother watched him she was sure he understood all she told him, with a knowledge beyond his years.

In late afternoons Samuel would often come in to rest because he was tired of playing and could run no more. Then his mother would take the Torah that belonged to Elkanah, and from the great parchment roll she would read to him the easier parts that would hold his interest. Then too the look of far wisdom came over his face; he seemed to hear deep, secret meanings in the ancient words of the parchment. On the holy Sabbath, when the family rested from all work, Elkanah would always take the Torah to study by himself, a few pages each week. Then Samuel began to sit near him quietly on the floor, his legs crossed. And no matter how hard or dull the words seemed, the little boy listened.

At last the time came for Hannah to take him to Shiloh. Young as he was, Samuel was old enough now to get along without his mother. In Shiloh, Eli the *kohen gadol* and his two grown sons would look after him. And so it was that one morning Elkanah harnessed the horses to the wagon, and taking along a servant, he rode off with Hannah and Samuel to the *mishkan*, the holy House of the Almighty. With them they took three young

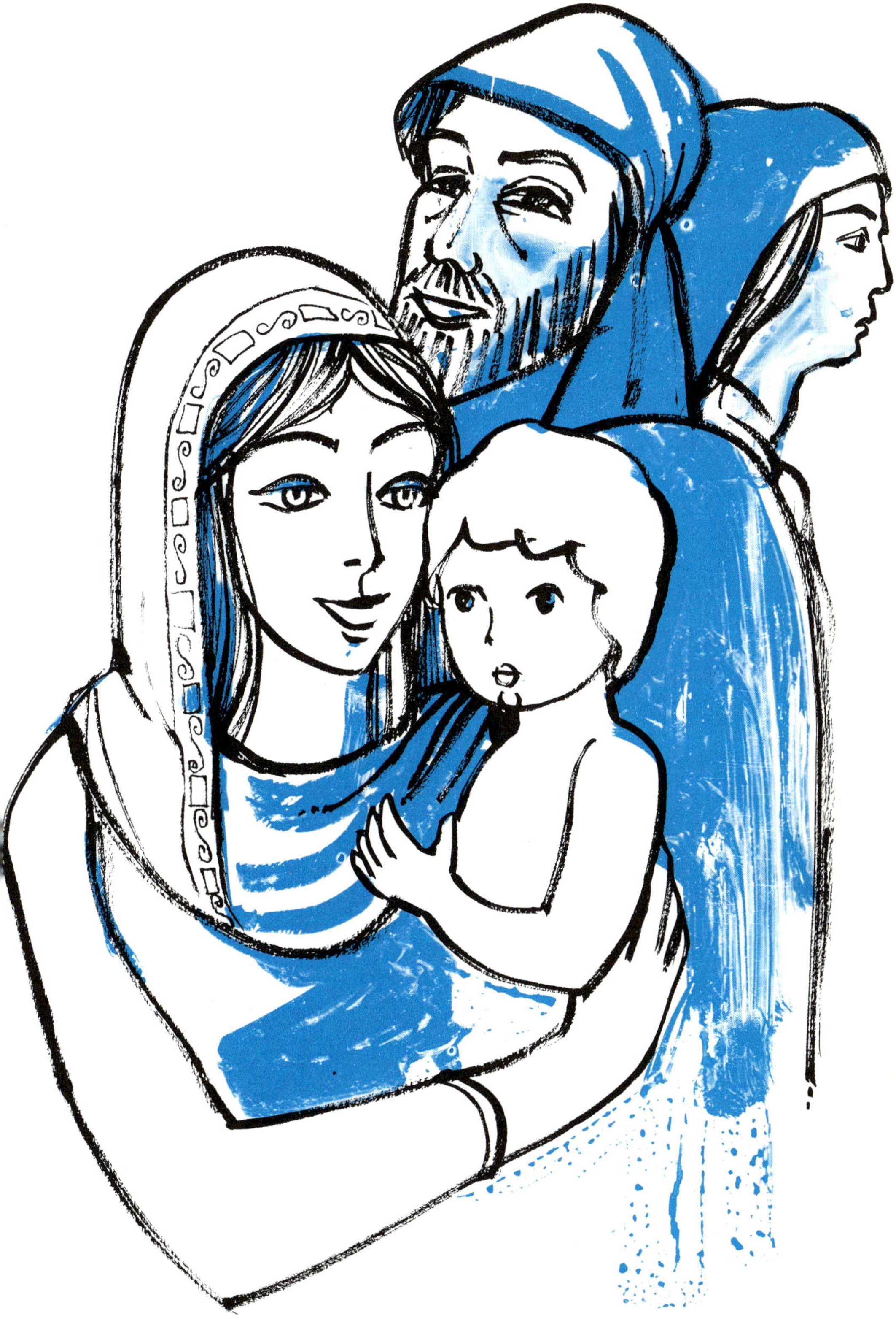

calves, a large measure of flour, and a leather bottle of wine — so that they would not only have food enough but would also be able to bring a sacrifice and an offering at the *mishkan*.

In the wagon, the father, mother and son were silent. Only once did Ḥannah ask Samuel, "Do you know where we are going, and why?"

"Yes, mother," answered the boy. "I know." And Ḥannah was sure he spoke the truth.

"Are you afraid?" she asked him.

"No, mother," he replied. "I am not afraid." And again she was sure he spoke the truth.

No Festival was approaching at this time of year, and there was hardly a person in Shiloh when they arrived. Leaving the servant to tend to the horses, Elkanah went with Ḥannah and Samuel to the *mishkan* at once, taking along a young calf to offer as a sacrifice.

Had it been the day before a Festival, hundreds of people would have been milling about before the *mishkan,* each waiting his turn to bring his offering. And Eli and his two sons would have been in the courtyard preparing and offering the many sacrifices. Now there was only one man standing idly in the courtyard.

"Sir," asked Elkanah, "are you a *kohen* who serves in this holy place? Perhaps you can offer up this young calf for us at the altar. We want to bring it as a sacrifice."

"I know how to prepare animals," said the man with a smile, "so that their meat may be used for kosher food. In my home town I always do that for my neighbors whenever any of them want kosher meat. But I am only an ordinary Israelite, not a *kohen*. Here you will have to wait for Eli or one of his sons. They seem to have gone away, but one of them will surely be back soon."

It was little Samuel who spoke up then, to the great surprise of all. Why he spoke, he himself did not know. Something within him made the words come. "Sir," said he, "you know how to prepare an animal so that its meat will be kosher?"

"Oh yes," the man replied.

"Then take this calf and prepare it," said Samuel, "but bear in mind that it is to be a holy sacrifice to the Almighty."

The man protested: "I tell you I am no *kohen*. Wait for Eli or one of his sons."

"And *I* tell you," said Samuel, "that we need not wait. Any Israelite may do as I say."

Afterward they would wonder why they ever listened to this little boy. But now some higher power or authority seemed to be speaking through his voice. Without question Elkanah led the young calf to the altar, and the man made the preparations as Samuel said.

And at that moment, Eli entered.

In the old man's voice there was cold fury, like ice that burned. "Sir, are you a *kohen*, that you do such things in the *mishkan*?"

"No," replied the man, suddenly afraid. "But this boy said it is permitted. He told me to do it."

"Which boy?" roared Eli. The man took little Samuel and led him forward; and Eli turned his angry eyes on the youngster. "Did you tell him that?" The boy nodded. "For what reason, then?" asked the old *kohen gadol*.

Again words came into Samuel's mind — from where, he did not know; but he knew he must speak them: "This is what is written in the Torah," he said; and to the amazement of all he recited by heart a difficult sentence from the Bible (Leviticus 1:5). Then Samuel continued: "The Torah tells us there of two things to be done when an animal is offered up as a sacrifice. The first is done before the altar, and the second at the altar. But it mentions a *kohen* only for the second part — at the altar. For the first part, then, no *kohen* is needed."

Eli heard the power and authority in the boy's voice — and the rightness in the boy's words. Thoughtfully he stroked his beard. "You speak well," he murmured. "I have never thought of that. I believe you are right . . ." Then his anger returned, and again his words were as a sword: "You may be right. Yet how did you dare to decide a matter of religious law here, at the *mishkan?* Here I am in authority. I alone may speak on such matters. Anyone else who decides here what may be done — deserves to die!"

A shudder went through Ḥannah, and she was truly

afraid. She knew Eli's power. One word from him, and great harm could befall her child. At Eli's feet she knelt. "O my lord!" she cried. "As your spirit lives, my lord, I am the woman who stood before you here to pray to the Eternal Lord. It was in this very courtyard. Do you not remember? I am the one who wept because I had never had a child."

Eli stared at Ḥannah with a long puzzled look. He did not remember her. Then, slowly, a picture rose in his mind of a woman standing a long time, whispering, as the tears streamed down her face. "Yes," he said softly; "yes."

"You gave me your blessing then," said Ḥannah, "and you promised that my prayer would be answered. Well, it was for a child I prayed. And now you would ask the Almighty to harm his life?" Amid her tears her voice was shrill with fear. "Have mercy on him!"

Still Eli's anger would not leave him. "I prayed once for you," said he, "and my prayer was granted. I will ask of the Almighty and he will give you another son, a better son, in his place. Let me be, for I must punish him."

"It was for *this* child I prayed," exclaimed Ḥannah; "and the Eternal Lord granted my plea that I begged of Him." Suddenly a bold thought came to her, and she rose to her feet. "Furthermore," she continued, "I have also lent him to the Lord. For all his life he is lent to the Lord. He is no plaything given to me because I prayed.

He is the Lord's own. Would you dare bring his death?"

Another memory came now to Eli. There had been the heavenly echo that a great prophet would be born in Israel. He himself had thought that this very woman would probably be the mother. So Samuel was destined to be a mighty prophet, for all he knew. Perhaps, thought Eli, that was why the boy had spoken so boldly — because Heaven had told him what to say.

Gone was the anger from Eli now. "I do remember you well now," said he. "Bring the boy to me." Bending slightly, he took the little Samuel by the hand and kissed him on the forehead. "Are you ready to come and live with me near this holy place? You will learn to help me take care of it." Samuel nodded: "I will stay with you. My mother has explained it all to me." Tenderly he kissed his father and mother farewell. Then, just before he went off with Eli, he quickly bowed down (as he had seen the grown-ups do) before the Almighty whom he would serve for the rest of his life.

With tears in their eyes, Elkanah and Ḥannah watched him, until he was gone from their sight.

Elkanah went back to the wagon, but Ḥannah stayed behind a bit. Once more she stood alone in the courtyard and whispered silently to the Almighty. This time, though, there were no tears. "There is no one holy as the Eternal Lord," she prayed, "for there is no one else but You, and there is no rock of strength like our God." She gave thanks and praise with all her heart.

6

GROWING UP IN SHILOH

A new world opened for Samuel — the world of the little sanctuary that they called the *mishkan*. There was no time here to romp and play. From every part of Israel people came every day, bringing animals for sacrifices and flour and wine for offerings. Eli and his two sons were kept busy from morning till night. And it was Samuel's duty to help Eli.

He learned to carry the vessels and tools that Eli used for the offerings. He came to know all the special garments that Eli had to wear, some of pure white linen, some with spun gold woven into the threads. In time he was able to keep all the garments in neat order, and he knew which ones to bring just when Eli, as the *kohen gadol*, would need them. And finally he learned to pour water from the copper basin on his old master's hands and feet (the ground of the *mishkan* was holy, and no one was allowed to walk about there in shoes — just as the Almighty had told Moses to remove his shoes before the burning bush). This washing made Eli ready for his duties in the *mishkan,* to do the many things that only a *kohen* might do.

Many a time Eli entered the holy chambers of the *mishkan*. Then Samuel remained strictly outside, knowing it was forbidden for him to go within.

Eli was a kindly taskmaster and a patient teacher. Never again did he grow angry with little Samuel; nor did he mention any more how Samuel had once made him furious. In time the two grew to have a great liking for each other.

One day, when Samuel had been there only a short while, the old *kohen gadol* suddenly asked him, "Tell me, my child: Do you like being here?"

"Indeed I do," said Samuel; "indeed I do. And yet there are times when I feel a great longing to be back home, with my mother and father."

"That is a natural feeling, to be expected. As you get older, it will leave you. What you must remember is that you truly belong here — not just because your mother promised you to the Almighty before you were born, but because you are, like your father, a member of the tribe of Levi. You see, Moses and his brother Aaron were of the tribe of Levi too. Aaron became the first *kohen,* in the *mishkan* that the Hebrews built in the wilderness; and everyone who is born into Aaron's family line is a *kohen* in turn. But everyone else of the tribe of Levi has a duty to help in this sanctuary, just as you are doing."

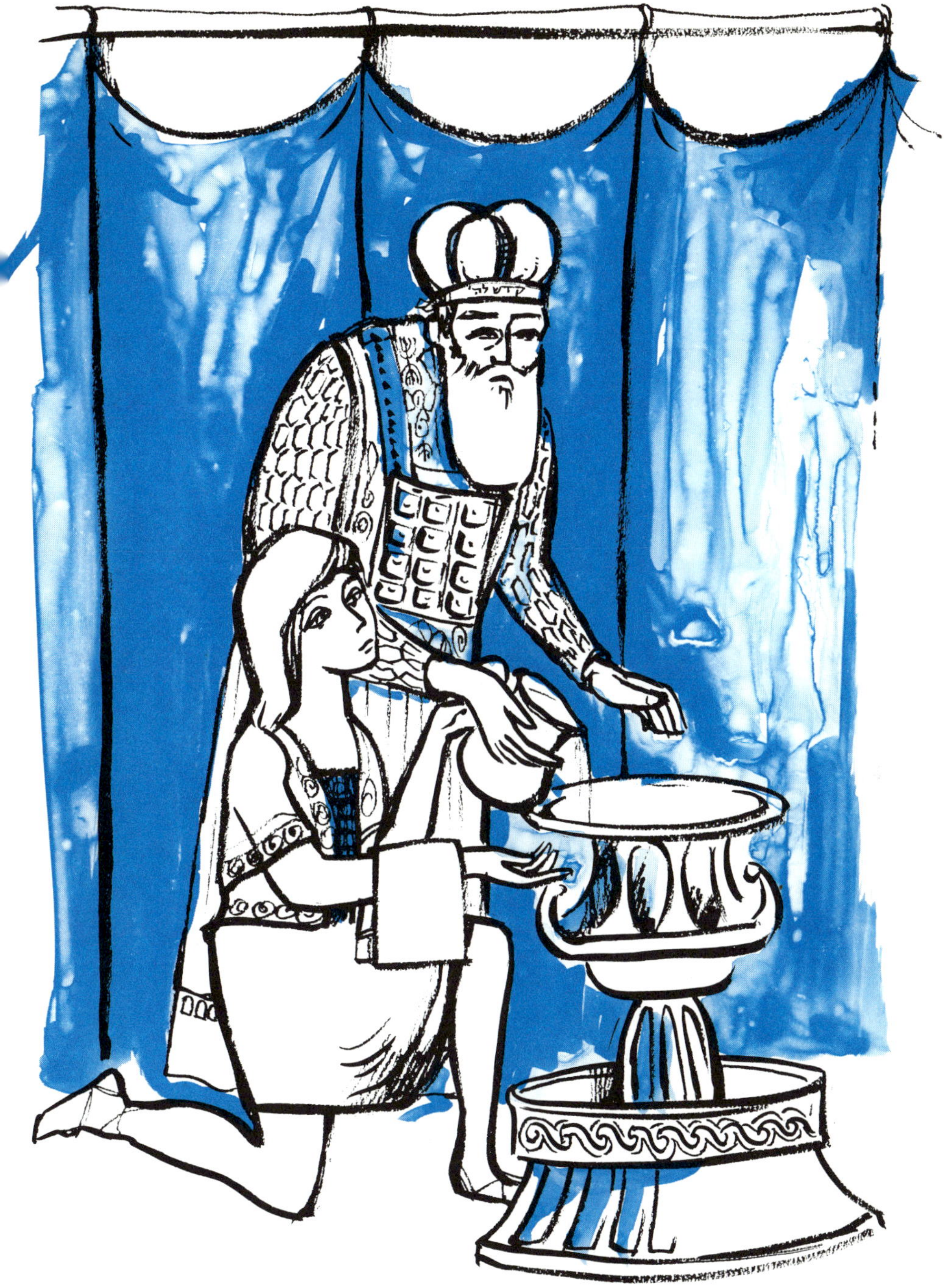
קדש לה'

"Then why," asked the boy Samuel, "is there no other *kohen* here except you and your two sons? And why am I the only one helping you?"

"There have been others in the past," Eli replied. "Perhaps others will come in the future. You see, mostly they do not know the laws of the Torah that would tell them what to do. And they busy themselves with farms and cattle to make sure they will have food to eat. But never you fear, my child. It will not be always like this. There is a vision that comes to me from time to time, so strong and clear that I know it is a prophecy. Some day it will come true. I see our people all settled and safe from enemies. At their head is a wise and powerful king. And in place of this little *mishkan* there will be then a splendid Temple of dazzling white and gold." As the old *kohen gadol* spoke, Samuel began to picture the Temple with him.

"In that Temple," continued Eli, "I see not one *kohen* or three, but hundreds. There will be so many that they will take turns: Every week a different group will come to serve. And many more hundreds of the tribe of Levi will be there to help them. At special times they will sing and play music. Perhaps it will not happen while you and I are living. But some day it will happen."

In Samuel's face there was an eager look: "You said the people of Levi would sing and play music sometimes. Should I do that here too? Can you teach me to sing and play instruments?"

"Perhaps," said Eli softly, "perhaps . . . all in good time. There is something far more important which you must learn first: the Torah which the Almighty gave to Moses. As long as you work at the *mishkan,* people will expect you to know it and to answer their many questions about it. We will study together for an hour a day."

Samuel was kept busy, and the days and weeks fled swiftly by. About one thing, he found, Eli was quite right: The more time that passed, the less often he felt a deep longing to be back home. He was beginning to think of this place in Shiloh as home.

At night, though, the feeling came back sometimes, stronger than ever. Next to the holy chamber of the *mishkan,* a little building of two rooms had been added long ago. In the first room, the living quarters for *kohanim,* Eli slept. In the second room, for people of the tribe of Levi, stood Samuel's bed. And whenever he went to bed, he noticed how very, very still it was. Back home, with Peninnah's ten boys, there had always been noise — talking, giggling, romping — until he fell asleep. Now, when it was so utterly still at the *mishkan,* tears came to his eyes sometimes, and he wished with all his heart to be back in his parents' house in Ramah.

But then he began to look out his window, and he noticed a soft glowing light, coming from the *mishkan,* He had never been inside, where only a *kohen* might go. But from the Torah that Eli was teaching him, he knew what was making the soft lovely glow. It was the *menorah,* the great lamp of seven lights, that Eli filled with the purest olive oil every evening, and lit the wicks that would burn till morning.

Through his window, Samuel watched the *menorah's* holy light; and he stopped feeling homesick and lonely. For some reason he could not understand, that soft glow in the dark of night soothed and comforted him, until he fell asleep peacefully. In time he never felt homesick at night either.

As much as he liked helping Eli in his duties, the young Samuel loved even more the hours they spent together in Eli's room studying the *kohen gadol's* great parchment scroll of the Torah. The boy's eyes followed the written words carefully, as the aged Eli read aloud and explained. Once, on a cloudy afternoon, the light grew dim, until Samuel could barely make out the words. He looked up at Eli, and found the old man gazing at a wall, not looking at the parchment at all. Yet the *kohen gadol* read the words aloud perfectly, without a mistake.

"Master," said Samuel, "you do not look at the Torah."

"No, my child. At times my eyes grow weak with age, and I cannot see the words."

"But you read it aloud so exactly," said the boy in wonder. "How do you know it so well?"

"Years ago I wrote this scroll myself, and I have

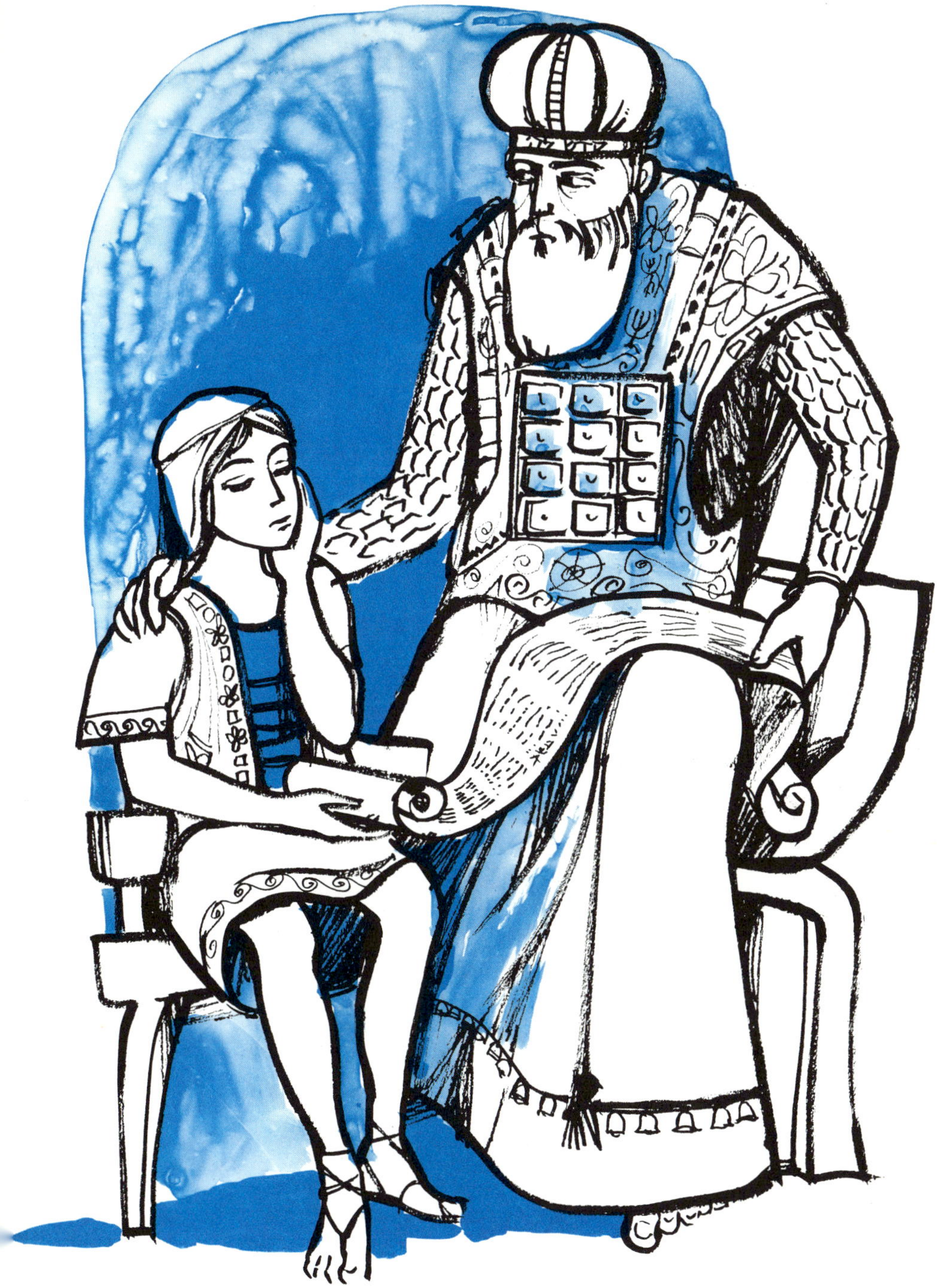

studied it many times since. . . . Do you know how I wrote it? You read in this Torah that when Moses took the Hebrews out of Egypt, the Almighty divided the Red Sea, and they crossed over on dry land. Well, when Joshua led the next generation of Hebrews out of the wilderness into this land, the Almighty divided the Jordan River, and they too went over on dry land. As they went across, they took along twelve great stones from the river bed. Later they made a huge altar of the stones in Gilgal; they plastered the altar with white lime, and on it they wrote the entire Torah, exactly as Moses had given it to them."

Eli paused a moment to catch his breath. Then his voice rose again, as daylight began fading from the room before the shadows of evening:

"Already in the wilderness, while Moses was alive, the Almighty commanded our people to do this. Once across the Jordan River, they were to make an altar of twelve great stones, cover it with plaster, and write on it the entire Torah. Do you know why?" Samuel gave no answer; and Eli continued: "Joshua would have to lead the people through many battles until they conquered this land that the Almighty promised us. Then they would be busy dividing the land, until each one had his farm or pasture. Would anyone be able to study the Torah in all that time? Would anyone even keep a scroll of it safe and sound through all the days of upheaval? While they fought to conquer the land and worked to settle it, the Torah would be forgotten and lost. So it was written on an altar of stones away off in Gilgal." Again the old *kohen gadol* paused to catch his breath.

"When I became the chief *kohen,* in charge of this *mishkan,* I could hardly find a good copy of the entire Torah — only sections and pieces. Oh, yes — some had complete scrolls of the Torah; it was not entirely forgotten. Your own father has one. But try as I would, I could find no person to sell me one or write one for me. I prepared the finest parchment I could get, and went down to Gilgal. There I sat for weeks upon weeks, copying the Torah letter by letter, line by line, from the white altar of the twelve stones. That copy which I made, is the one we are now studying."

In the rapidly darkening room the silence waited for him to speak again.

"Take care, my child," said the aged Eli, "to study it until you too can read every word from your mind. The time may come when you alone will know it in Israel, and you will have to teach it to our people."

Samuel wanted to ask about Eli's own two grown sons, Ḥophni and Pinḥas. Surely they had learned the Torah from him; surely they could teach it too. But he said nothing. He had already noticed that they were not always good sons to their aged father. And he decided to remain silent.

Not long afterward, the day came when Samuel

knew that he had learned his duties well. For Eli gave him a tunic of fine linen, a special garment to wear over his other clothing — a uniform that would mark him as a full-fledged servant of the Almighty at the *mishkan*. When he first put it on, his heart was glad. And how proud his mother and father were to see him in it when another Festival came and they arrived once more in Shiloh with family and kinsmen.

"You look so fine in that tunic," said Ḥannah, as he stood among his wondering and admiring family. "Do you miss us at all?" she asked. "Do you wish sometimes that you could come back to us?"

"I did at first," said Samuel, "but not any more. I know I belong here." And then the words came pouring from him, as he eagerly told his mother (and his family) all that happened since they had left him there.

Ḥannah was thankful. With love and tenderness she draped a little coat about his shoulders. "I have made this for you," she said. "It will be good to wear when the days grow colder." And then the boy and his parents went to see Eli, seated in his chair in the sanctuary courtyard.

The aged *kohen gadol* smiled with pleasure. "May you be blessed," said he to Ḥannah, "that you have lent this lad to the Almighty — and to me. He is a great comfort to me as I now grow older. How can I ever pay you back? . . . I think I know . . . Tell me: do you not feel lonely again, without your little son — as though you were childless once more?" All at once he rose from his chair and turned to Elkanah: "May the Eternal Lord give you more children from this woman, in return for the one that has been lent to the Lord."

In the next few years, whenever Ḥannah came to Shiloh at Festival time, she always brought along a little coat that she had made. Each coat was a bit larger than the one before, to fit Samuel's growing body. And each time, when they came before the aged Eli, he blessed Ḥannah that she should have more children, in place of the one she had left with him. "Let your new children bring joy to you," said he, "as Samuel brings comfort to me."

Eli's blessing was fulfilled, and over the years Ḥannah gave birth to three sons and two daughters. But these children brought not only joy to Elkanah's house; they brought tragedy also.

Ever since Ḥannah had given birth to Samuel, Peninnah had stopped teasing and taunting her with cruel words. But she remained jealous and bitter, filled with hate. Never once did she think to ask Ḥannah to forgive her for all the times she had made her rival suffer. And she trained her boys to be as cruel as she was.

It is told that Heaven may wait a long time before it makes a person pay for bad and wicked deeds — but Heaven never forgets, and it finds its own time to settle accounts.

As Ḥannah began to bear her new children (the three sons and two daughters), Peninnah's children began to die off. The first year that Ḥannah had a new child, two of Peninnah's youngsters took sick and passed away. Peninnah thought it was merely an accident, or bad luck. The next year another child was born to Ḥannah, and another two children of Peninnah's took sick and died. Still Peninnah thought it was only bad luck, nothing more. But the same thing happened the third year, and again the fourth year. Now Ḥannah had four children aside from Samuel, and of Peninnah's ten sons eight had died; only two were left.

At last Peninnah understood that Heaven's will was at work here: she was paying dearly for her cruelty. And at last she was frightened.

When it became clear that Ḥannah would soon give birth to a fifth child, Peninnah fell to her knees before her. "Have mercy on me," she cried. "Every time a new baby is born to you, two of mine die! I know it is Heaven's punishment because I was always so spiteful to you. But eight of my children are dead. Now you are going to have another one — and Heaven will take my last two. I will have no children left! Pray for me, Ḥannah. Pray for the last two children I have." And she wept bitter tears.

Ḥannah prayed long and earnestly; that year there were no deaths in the family. And never again was Peninnah cruel or spiteful.

7

SONS OF EVIL

The older Samuel grew, the more respected and beloved he was, both by the Almighty and by the people who came to Shiloh. He went about his work quietly and happily. But with each passing year Eli became weaker, and the day came when little Samuel began to help him also to dress and to eat.

It did not take the boy long to find out that something very wrong was going on now at the *mishkan*. As long as his strength had lasted, Eli had gone often to the altar and the courtyard, to watch that all went well. And with their father about, his sons Ḥophni and Pinḥas did their work properly. But now that he was weaker, the aged *kohen gadol* spent more and more time in his room, and Ḥophni and Pinḥas could do as they pleased. They were greedy men, and in their greed they became evil.

One day, when Samuel had nothing to do because Eli was resting, the boy put on his plain clothing and went out to see what was going on. It was a day when many came to the *mishkan* to bring offerings. Unnoticed,

Samuel went about among them, to see what the two grown sons of Eli did.

In a few moments the boy began to notice the two servants of Ḥophni and Pinḥas going about among the people, pulling along a huge tub on a little platform with wheels; and one servant carried a very large fork with three teeth or prongs.

One man was cutting up the meat of a lamb that had just been offered as a sacrifice, as he prepared to boil it for himself and his family. The servants stopped near him. "That is a fine sheep you have there," said one servant with a laugh. "Let us have a piece for Ḥophni the *kohen*."

"What do you mean?" asked the Israelite. "Do you not know the Torah's law? There are things that Ḥophni must still do at the altar to make this a good, proper sacrifice, accepable to the Almighty. Afterward I must give him two choice portions of this meat, which the Torah names, and nothing more. That is the law."

"Ḥophni and Pinḥas have their own laws," said the servant, a touch of temper in his voice. "You want Hophni to do at the altar all he is supposed to, to make your sacrifice proper and acceptable. Is that not right? You would not want him to forget about it, would you?"

"No, no!" exclaimed the Israelite. "Then the sacrifice would be worthless. It would only make the Almighty angry. They must do as the Torah says!"

"Very well," said the servant, holding out his hands.

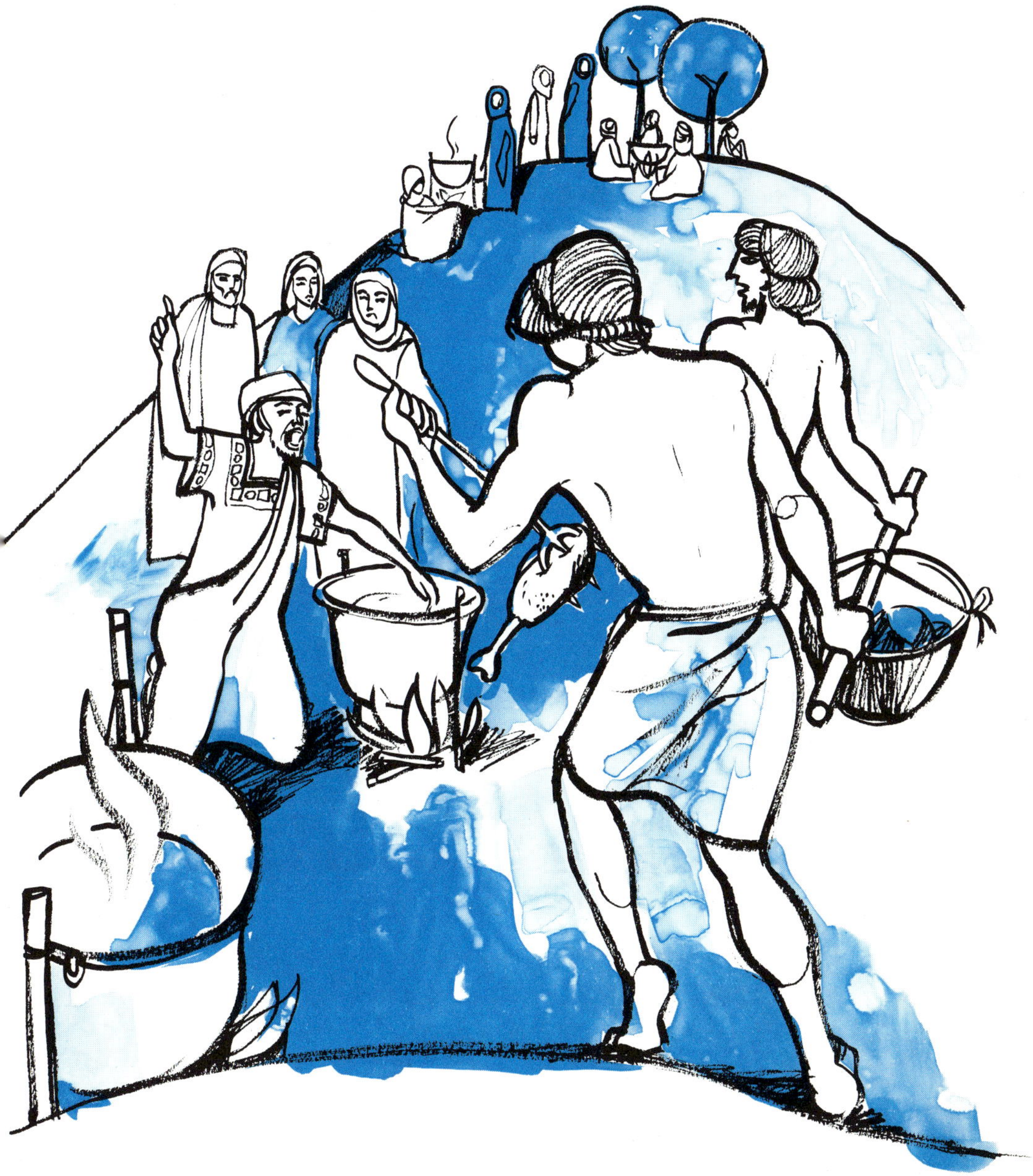

"Then let us have a large, handsome piece of meat for my master to roast, and he will gladly do all you wish."

With an angry mutter the man threw a piece into the other's hands. In it went into the huge tub, and the servants moved on, their cruel laughter ringing in the air. They stopped before a large pot in which meat was already boiling. Now the second servant lifted his giant three-pronged fork and thrust it hard into the pot.

"What are you doing?" cried a man with a short beard. "That is my meat." And the servant answered with a sneer, "Do you not know the law of Ḥophni and Pinḥas? Whatever comes up on this fork belongs to them."

"And is the Torah's law not enough for them?" asked the man. "Can they not be content with the portions that the Almighty bids us give them when our cooking is done?"

"Indeed no," the servant laughed. "They have large appetites." He needed both hands to lift the meat that came out on the fork. Hardly anything was left in the pot.

"But I need this meat," pleaded the man, "to feed my children until we return home. You leave me so little that we will starve!"

"That is no concern of ours," said the other. "You can always beg food from others."

So the servants went among the Israelites. If anyone refused to give them what they wanted, they would attack him together and take it by force.

Samuel could hardly believe his eyes and ears. The sacrifices were supposed to be something holy. When a man's offering was brought the right way, as the Torah taught, the man could then pray to the Creator of heaven and earth, and his prayer would be answered. If the sacrifices were right, Heaven forgave a man his sins. Now everything was all wrong. Ḥophni and Pinḥas cared nothing about the Almighty and His Torah. They thought only of their own pleasure and greed.

Samuel's heart was troubled. No good would come of it all, he knew. Yet to the aged Eli, who hardly came to the courtyard any more, the boy said nothing. He was wise enough to know that Eli's sons would never heed a word of their pious father. If he told Eli what Ḥophni and Pinḥas were doing, the old man would only be saddened by an aching heart, and nothing would be changed. Samuel kept still and did his duties just as before.

Yet soon Eli knew all the evil that his sons were doing. Among the Israelites who came to Shiloh for every Festival, a few had become close friends with him over the years. Before they left Shiloh to return to their village, they would always visit the *kohen gadol* for a good talk. After the next Festival, however, they came to bid him farewell and to tell him sadly that they would not be back in Shiloh any more.

"But why?" asked the astonished Eli. One of the men answered: "When you took care of our sacrifices, we loved to come. We could feel the holiness here, like the warming rays of the sun. We knew the Almighty was pleased with us, and He would make our farmland prosper. But now your sons make us sorry we come. No one feels any holiness here any more. The very air is filled with anger. We think it will be better for us to stay at home and pray alone to the Almighty." And they told Eli all that Ḥophni and Pinḥas were doing.

As the day wore on, others also came to pay their respects to the aged Eli. He asked them questions, and from their answers he knew that his old friends had spoken only the truth: His sons had turned evil.

As soon as he could, Eli sent for his sons. Perhaps he could make them change, he thought hopefully. When they stood before him, he spoke: "Why do you do such things?" he asked gently. "From everyone I hear of your bad deeds. No, my sons: It is not good, what I hear the people of the Lord saying about you." There was cold hate in the faces of Hophni and Pinhas. But Eli's eyes were too old to see it, and he spoke on:

"If a man does wrong only to another man, God will judge him. The Almighty's court of law will settle the matter between the two people, and all will be well again. But if a man sins against the Eternal Lord, who will plead and pray for him? Who will ask Heaven to be kind to him? No one. And Heaven's punishment will be swift and sure. . . . Take care, my sons," Eli pleaded. "You are harming the people who come here — but perhaps they will forgive you, and all will be well. Yet what you are doing is also a great sin against the Almighty. Change your ways now, before it is too late — before Heaven sets its punishment." And his sons said nothing.

The aged Eli could not see their faces clearly. He hoped his words had softened their hearts. But from his corner, where he sat quietly, Samuel watched them, and he knew they were laughing at their father as a silly old fool. "Change," said Eli again to them. "Stop your evil ways."

"It is too soon, dear father," they replied. "Now we are young, and we want to enjoy ourselves. When we are old, like you, it will be time enough to become pious and good."

Suddenly Samuel knew that Heaven had already decided what would happen to them. They would never have a chance to grow old.

One bright morning, as the boy Samuel left his room to go about his work, he was startled to see Elkanah his father. "Why have you come, father?" he asked. "I did not expect you until the next Festival." Elkanah's face was sad and troubled. "I cannot talk with you now," he replied. "I have had a message from the Almighty, and I must speak with Eli." He strode on to the old man's room.

When Eli heard Elkanah's voice, his face lit up with a smile. But as Elkanah spoke, the smile vanished.

"Forgive me," said Samuel's father, "for what I must say to you. I have had a message from the Almighty, which I am commanded to give you. It is not a happy thing I must tell you."

"I understand," said Eli softly. "I myself used to hear the word of the Lord ever so often. Sometimes it told of good things to come, sometimes of bad things. Now that I am old, the Almighty's messages do not reach me any more. But if you have heard a Divine prophecy, tell it to me without fear. You must, or you will have no peace." And he waited in silence, until Elkanah spoke:

"This is what the Eternal Lord says to you: I revealed Myself to your forefather's house, your people, when they were yet in Egypt, slaves in Pharaoh's domain. And I chose him — your forefather Aaron — out of all the tribes of Israel, to be my *kohen,* to offer sacrifices on My altar . . . As I chose him, so I chose his sons and grandsons and great-grandsons — and you yourself, and your sons. All of you were to be holy, to serve Me and honor Me as I have commanded. Why then do your sons kick out in scorn at My sacrifices and My offerings, which I have ordered in My dwelling? You have honored your sons above Me, fattening them on the first, choicest parts of the offerings of Israel My people. And they have brought shame and disgrace on the worship of the Eternal Lord."

Eli closed his eyes. He knew there would be punishment from Heaven because his sons were greedily disobeying the Torah in the Almighty's own sanctuary. But why did the Almighty say that he, Eli, gave his sons the first, choicest parts of the sacrifices? They did that themselves now, against his will, taking far more than their just share. Why did the Almighty's words, that Elkanah spoke, put the blame on him?

Then Eli remembered: When his sons were little, they would often roam about the courtyard to watch the people cooking the meat of their sacrifices. And they would beg for tidbits to eat, before Eli had finished his duties at the altar. He remembered: he had thought it harmless, even charming, and never had he stopped them. He had always been too kind to his sons, never strict, never punishing. He had thought the holiness of the *mishkan* would make them good. It was indeed his fault that now they were evil.

All this went swiftly through his mind, in the space of a few seconds. Then Elkanah spoke again, giving the message he had heard:

"Therefore the Lord God of Israel declares: I said indeed that your father's people and yours should walk before Me as My ministers for ever. But now the Lord says: it would be a disgrace for Me; for those who know Me, I will honor; and those who despise Me shall find contempt."

Then Elkanah's voice rose with the Almighty's words: "Behold, the days are coming when I will cut off the strength of your arm and of your father's house, so that none in your house shall reach old age. You shall see distress in your dwelling, amid all the good that Israel will have; and nevermore shall anyone in your house become an elder, in honor and respect. . . . And this shall be the sign for you — that it will come true: a fate shall befall your two sons, Ḥophni and Pinḥas, that in one day both shall die. And I will appoint for Me a faithful *kohen,* who will act according to My heart and spirit; and I will build him a safe house . . . And whoever is left of your house will come to bow down humbly before him for a piece of silver or a loaf of bread; and he will say: Take me in, I pray you, with one of the groups of *kohanim,* that I may have a morsel of bread to eat!"

Alone in the gathering darkness Eli sat on after Elkanah left, with tears in his eyes. He remembered well that in all their years as children, Ḥophni and Pinḥas had done little things that were bad — and he had done nothing. He had always thought time would change them. Now there was no more time. Heaven had already passed sentence.

Only the thought of Samuel was a comfort. The boy was as a true son to him. And Eli realized anew how loyal and religious young Samuel was: All this time the boy must have seen what Ḥophni and Pinḥas were doing. He could easily have joined them and become as greedy and wicked as they. Yet he remained what Ḥannah his mother had vowed he would be: a servant of the Almighty.

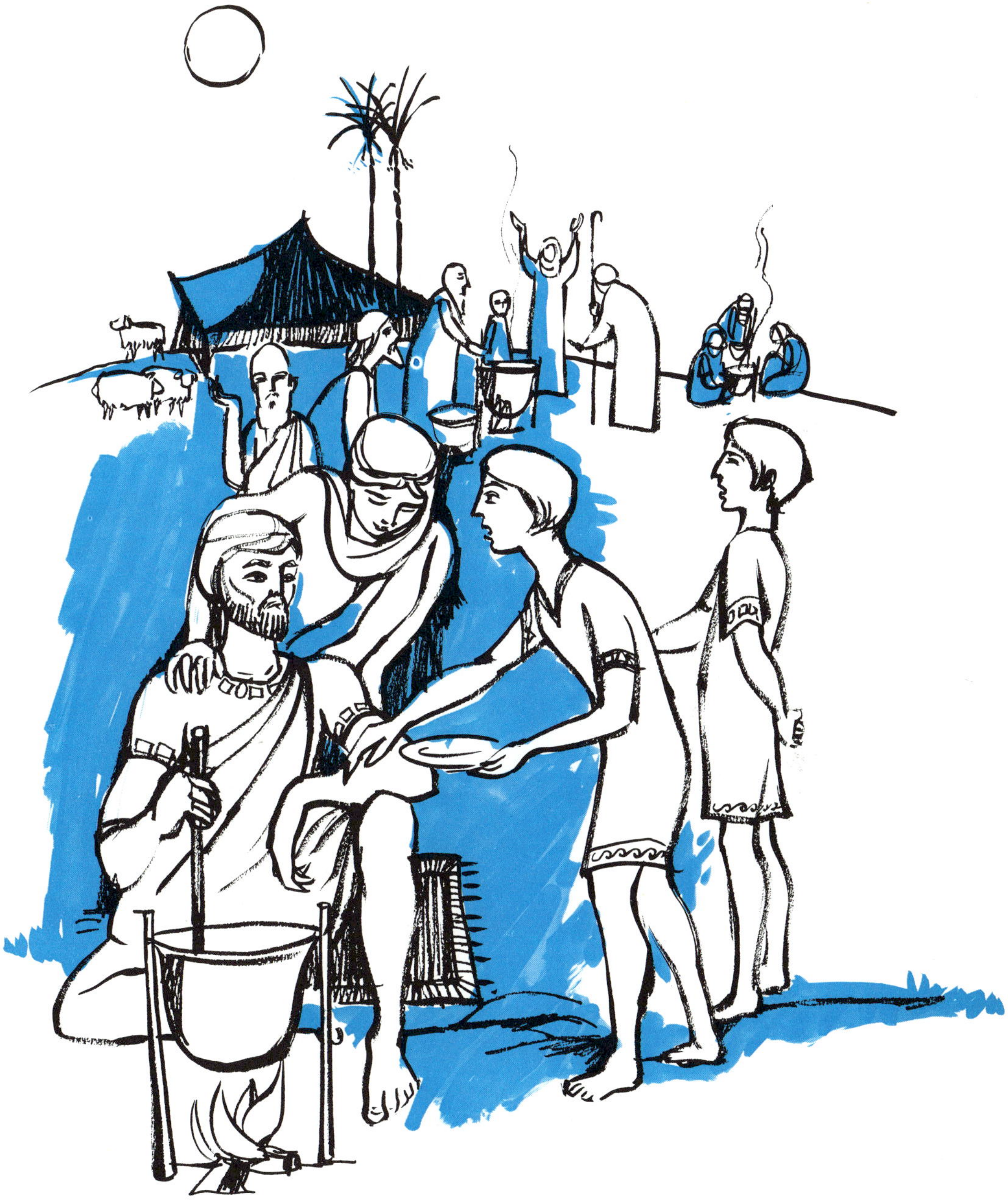

8

THE VOICE FROM THE ARK

The months passed one after the other, as the brown leaves fell in the dismal chill of late autumn. To Samuel it seemed that the very air was waiting and watching — for what, he did not know.

Actually, it was Heaven that was waiting and watching — to see what Eli and the Israelites would do about his two evil sons at the *mishkan*. Eli need not have sat in his room giving way to despair. Old and half blind as he was, he could yet go to the courtyard to stand by the altar and denounce his sons — speak out sternly and clearly against them. If he did that for several days, Ḥophni and Pinḥas would not dare continue their wicked deeds in his presence. They would simply leave and never return. Then at least the Almighty would no longer be scorned and dishonored in His own house of holiness.

But Eli was weak of spirit. In his heart he yet loved his sons as though they were little children still. He could not bear to shame them before the people and drive them away. Perhaps, he thought, if he only prayed for them, all would yet be well, and Heaven would not do the dreadful things that Elkanah had foretold.

And so it was that even after Elkanah's warning, Eli cared more for the love and honor of his sons than for the honor of the Almighty. Heaven waited and watched — and Heaven saw.

The Israelites too could have acted. Some knew it was better to stay away and bring no more sacrifices to the *mishkan,* since the Almighty was only being dishonored and disgraced there. But all the others continued to come. In Shiloh they had a carefree holiday, time to enjoy themselves. What did they care if Hophni and Pinhas were doing wrong? Had all stayed away, Eli's sons would have been forced to leave the *mishkan* for good. But the Israelites cared more for their pleasures in Shiloh than for the Almighty's honor. This too Heaven saw, as it waited and watched.

Until that time there were always people in Israel with the gift of prophecy. Every once in a while they would see a vision or hear a voice from Heaven, which let them know what was to happen and what the Israelites should do. They would tell everyone, and the Israelites would listen.

Now, as late fall gave way to cold winter, hardly anyone received any messages from Heaven. In all the land of Israel, barely a word of prophecy was heard.

All was dark and still as Eli slept in his room near

the holy chambers, and Samuel slept in the room beyond. Soon it would be dawn, on the day when Samuel would be thirteen years of age. Before he fell asleep he had thought about it. At thirteen he would no longer be a child. He would carry his own responsibility for obeying the laws and commandments of the Torah. Well, he thought before sleep came, he felt ready for that. Now the dark night moved a little closer to dawn.

"Samuel! Samuel!"

The boy heard his name and sat up at once. "Eli must be calling me," he thought. For the old *kohen gadol's* eyes were now very poor, and he needed the lad's help more than ever. "Here I am," he called out. "I am coming." As Samuel stood up, he saw through his window the glow of the *menorah's* light. That meant it was not yet dawn, for by then the light went out.

The *menorah's* soft golden glow made Samuel feel proud of Eli. Old as the *kohen gadol* was, and barely able to see, Samuel still took him to the door of the holy chambers every day, just as evening came. With sure steps Eli went in alone; with steady practiced hands he cleaned the *menorah* and poured in fresh olive oil, enough to last the night; then he put in new wicks and lit the *menorah's* seven lights. This task was too sacred for Eli to leave to his wicked sons.

But now Samuel did not have time to think of all this, as he went at once to Eli. "Here I am," he said, "for you called me." Eli opened his eyes in the dark. "I did

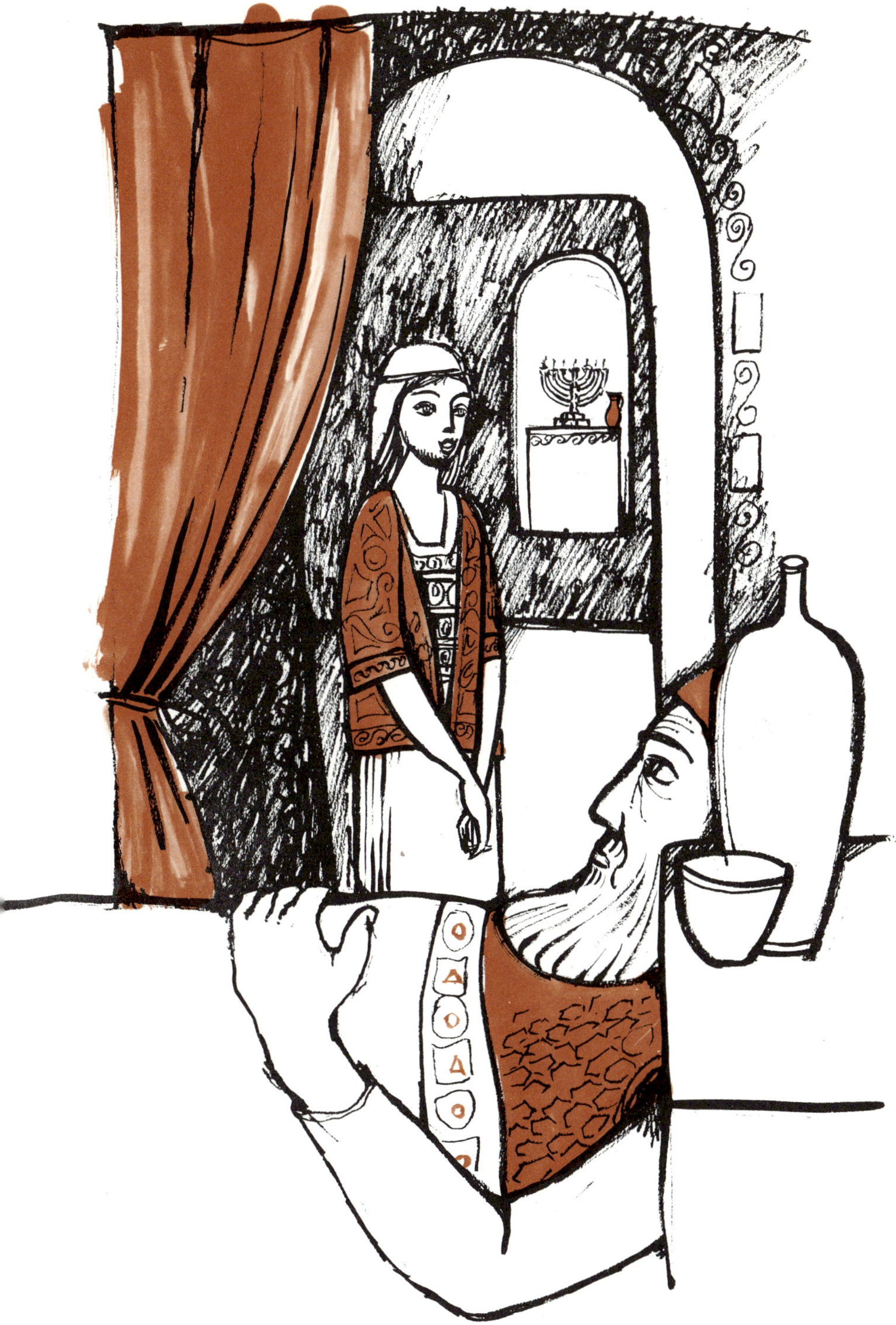

not call," he replied. "Go lie down again." And Samuel went back to bed, to wait for sleep to return.

"Samuel!"

Again he heard his name; and once more he went to Eli's bedside. "Here I am," he said again, "for you called me." But a puzzled Eli answered, "I did not call, my son. Perhaps you have been dreaming. Go lie down again."

Yet no sooner was the boy back in bed, alone in the dark stillness of his room, than he heard his name yet a third time. Back he went to Eli, and once more he said, "Here I am, for you called me."

Now Eli sat up. "Tell me, my son: These three times that you have been to see me, you really heard someone calling you?" Indeed yes, the boy replied: "I thought you wanted me to come and help you."

"No," said Eli, "it was not I. The voice you heard could have come from one place only. You know that my room is alongside the holy chamber where the *menorah* stands. Then there is a veil, an embroidered curtain, that hangs from the ceiling. Beyond the veil is another chamber — the Holy of Holies — and in it stands the holy ark, of which we have read in the Torah. It is a box of acacia wood set inside a larger box of gold; and within the acacia wood is yet another box, also of gold. That triple box contains the two tablets of sapphire stone on which the Almighty Himself wrote the Ten Commandments, that He gave to Moses.

"Now listen further," Eli continued. "On top of this ark are the cherubim, two little statues of gold, with the faces of infant children and the outspread wings of birds. The faces always look at each other in silent peace and holy innocence. As long as our people had the *mishkan* with them in the wilderness, do you know how Moses heard the words of the Almighty? There was always a voice that came from the place between the two cherubim. And only Moses heard that voice, no matter who stood nearby.

"If you hear a voice calling you now, it must come from the same place atop the ark in the Holy of Holies. My room is closer to it than yours — yet I have heard nothing. Do you know what that means? The Almighty is calling you. I have long known that you were meant to be a prophet, to hear His word and tell it. Because this is the very first time He is calling you, He has made the voice sound like mine, so that you would not be alarmed. Do not be afraid. Go lie down; and if He calls you again, say, *Speak, Lord, for Your servant is listening.*"

In a moment the boy was back in bed. His heart beat fast as he lay very still in the darkness before dawn, waiting. Then he heard the voice yet again: "Samuel, Samuel!" Without moving, he answered quietly, "Speak — be you some angel or the Almighty Himself — for Your servant is listening." And all at once he knew it *was* the Almighty, the Creator of the universe: Samuel could sense His divine presence in the room.

"Behold," said the voice: "I am about to do something in Israel so dreadful that whoever hears it, his two ears shall tingle. On that day I shall bring on against Eli all that I have foretold about his household, from beginning to end. I told him I would pass sentence on his house for ever, for the sin which he knew: for his sons are vile, heaping blasphemy and curse and disgrace on Me, and he did not restrain or stop them. Therefore I swear to the house of Eli that the guilt of Eli's house shall not be paid for by any sacrifice or offering, ever."

Now the room was still and quite empty. The Divine Presence was gone. Afraid and saddened at what he had heard, Samuel lay on his bed till morning came stealing softly into his room, and it was time for him to open the doors of the *mishkan*. The early sun was bright, but his heart remained dark with fear at the terrible future that the Almighty had shown him. So to Eli he said not a word; in fact, he kept away from his old master's room, fearing the questions his old master might ask.

But as the morning grew late, he heard Eli calling him gently, "Samuel, my son." The boy gathered his courage. "Here I am," he replied.

"What was it He said to you?" asked the *kohen gadol*; in his voice there was no fear or cringing. "Do not hide anything from me. If you keep anything back from me — even a word out of all He told you — so will God do to you, and more, as He promised to do to me. That is what happens to any prophet who keeps a prophecy to himself. You must remember that . . . Now speak; I am not afraid."

Eli was silent and thoughtful as Samuel told him all, leaving nothing out. Then the aged *kohen gadol* breathed out a long sigh: "That was the Eternal Lord who spoke. Can a vessel complain to the potter who made it? Even so can I say nothing to my Maker when He takes away what He has given me. Let Him do what is good in His sight, for He is a true judge, ever just and fair. Go now in peace, my son, and let me be."

9

WAR WITH THE PHILISTINES

As Samuel grew to manhood with the passing years, it did not take people long to discover that he had the gift of prophecy, so that he always knew the Almighty's will. Many times he heard the voice that came from the space between the two cherubim atop the holy ark. When he did not hear the voice, he had only to look into the stillness of his own heart, and he knew how to act and how to speak. Whenever he gave someone advice, his words were sound and good, filled with a wisdom beyond his years. Whenever he made a prediction to someone about his future, things happened later exactly as he foretold.

From one man to his neighbor the word spread; then from village to village, from town to town, and from city to city. Soon all Israel knew, from Dan to B'er-sheba, that the young lad who helped at the *mishkan* and took care of Eli was an excellent prophet of the Lord, and gifted with wisdom. Whatever he said was right and true. For years many had stayed away from Shiloh, unable to bear the behavior of Eli's sons. Now they came again, not to bring sacrifices, but to speak with young Samuel and listen to his growing wisdom.

Throughout the land, the Hebrews slept more soundly, without fear. They knew that in Shiloh there was a young lad who could lead them — by the word of the Almighty.

And while he was yet a youth, the elders of Israel came to him one day to ask a serious question: Should the Hebrews go to war?

On a narrow strip of land along the coast of the Mediterranean Sea lived the *p'lishtim,* called in English the Philistines. (From their name came the word *Palestine,* as a name for the land of Israel.) Long ago they had come by ship across the Mediterranean from Crete and the Aegean Islands — so that they were still called "the people of the sea." Now they lived in and around five strong fortified cities, each surrounded by a thick wall, and each ruled by a *seren,* a lord and master who was a first-rate military leader. (The title of *seren* came out of a Greek word from which we have the English word *tyrant.*) When Joshua had led the Hebrews to capture the land of Canaan, he could not drive the Philistines from their fortress cities. For the Philistines knew how to smelt iron to make strong armor, swift chariots, and sharp spears and swords.

Now the mighty Philistines no longer stayed in their five cities. Out they came in their red cloaks and plumed

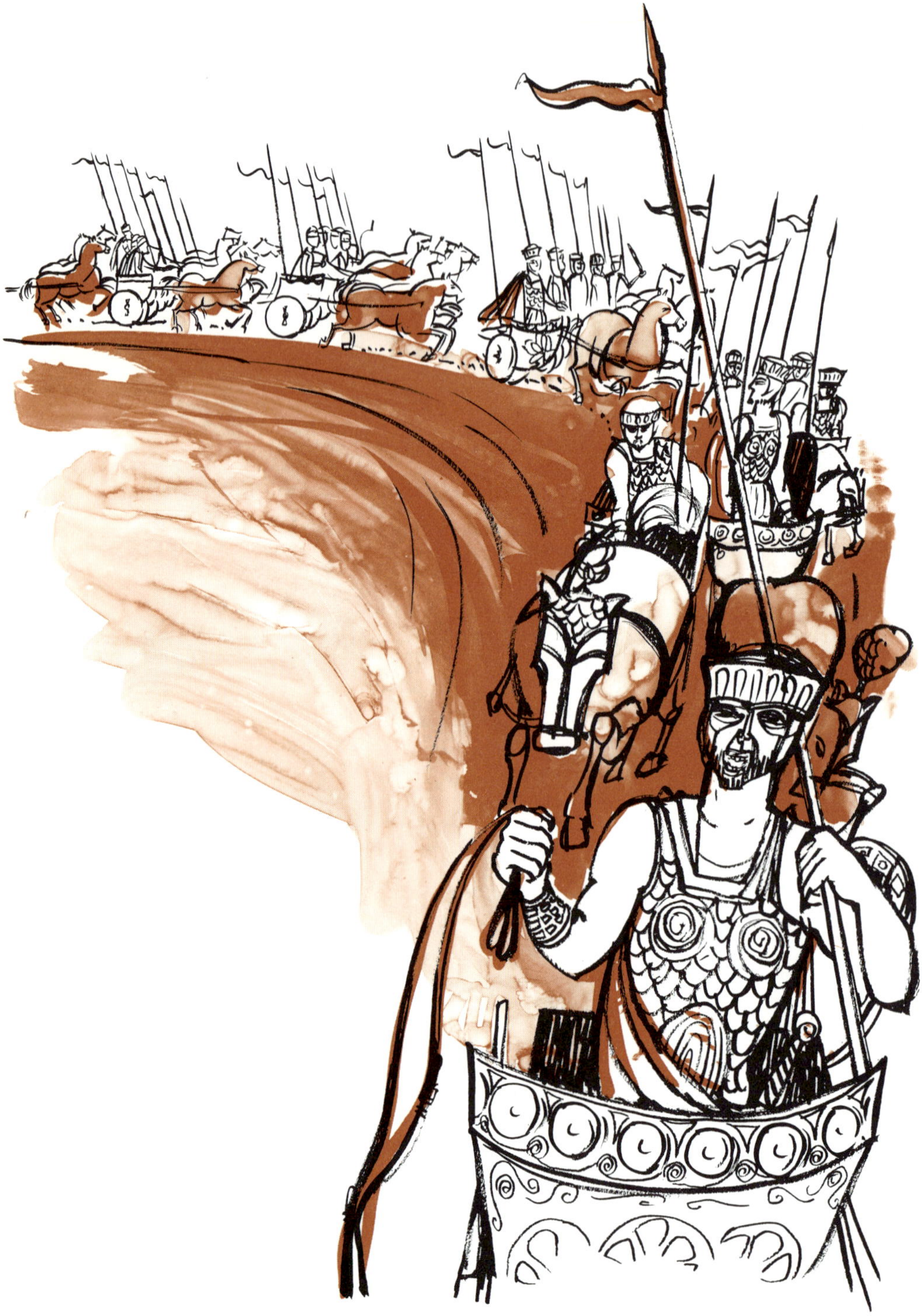

helmets, their green and purple banners flying from their chariots in the wind. They forced their way along the coastal plain, and on into the mountains in the territory of the tribe of Judah. The Hebrews had no chariots or horses, nor weapons of iron. They could not stop this enemy, that left soldiers in control of every town and village they took — soldiers who made the captive Hebrews live in misery as slaves.

In time the Philistines seized the approaches to the central mountains in the tribe of Ephraim's territory. When they captured parts of Ephraim's and Benjamin's territories where the Hebrews had felt safe in their mountain fastness since the days of Joshua, all Israel was alarmed and frightened. And the elders of Israel came to Shiloh to ask the young Samuel: Should the entire people gather into an army and meet the Philistines in full battle? Could Israel drive this fearsome enemy out?

Samuel closed his eyes and sat in silence. Yes, he said at last: Let the Hebrews wage war. With the Almighty helping them, they could win.

Northeast the Philistine army marched, to the slopes of Aphek, that led to the territory of Benjamin. And there they made camp and settled down. The Hebrews united by the thousands opposite them at Eben-ezer, in the foothills of Ephraim. On the plain between them the two armies met in battle.

Before the iron chariots of the Philistines that could ride freely on the plain, the Hebrews were no match.

Valiantly though they fought on their feet, they had only slings, bows and arrows, knives of flintstone, rocks and clubs — and their bare fists. Israel was defeated that day, and its army was forced back to the camp at Eben-ezer, leaving behind about four thousand dead.

Late in the night the Hebrew elders and chieftains met in the main tent of the army camp to consider what to do. "Why?" they asked. "Why did the Lord put us to rout today before the Philistines?" They knew they had done right to give battle—Samuel had told them to fight. Then why had the Almighty not given them courage to overcome the enemy's chariots, armor, and iron weapons? For a long while they sat in silence, seeking an answer. At last one elder spoke:

"It is because our people did not really feel, deep in their hearts, that the Almighty was with them. If they had truly felt Him on our side, each one would have fought with the strength of a hundred. With our bare hands we would have overturned their chariots and smashed their armor over their own heads."

"Then how shall we give our people courage?" asked a chieftain. "How shall we make them feel the Almighty is truly with them?"

"I know," said a third. "Let us bring something here that is the Almighty's very own possession, that is most closely and surely His . . ."

"Yes," said the elder, "that is a good idea . . . Let us bring here from Shiloh the holy ark—the ark of the Lord's covenant—so that He will come among us and save us from the might of our enemies." And to that all agreed. Once they had the ark with them, they were sure the Hebrews would fight twice as hard.

That very night they sent messengers to Shiloh to bring back the holiest object in all Israel—the box of acacia wood encased in gold, that contained the Ten Commandments in the two tablets of stone.

In the camp at Eben-ezer the Hebrew army slept soundly through the dark of night. Not one heard the heavenly echo that sighed in the wind: "When the sons of Eli angered Me by their vile deeds at the *mishkan,* you did not think of the holy ark—to make them stop disgracing it by their shameless sins. Now you think of the ark, when you want to win a battle."

Had the elders sent for Samuel, they would have learned at once why they had lost the day's battle and how they could triumph when they fought again. They lost because the Israelites were guilty of letting Eli's sons do as they pleased at the *mishkan.* They had only to admit their error and make a vow to drive Ḥophni and Pinḥas from the *mishkan,* and the Almighty would drive the enemy away, no matter how powerful the Philistines were.

But in the Hebrew camp all slept.

It was bright morning when the army messengers arrived at the *mishkan,* just as Samuel was opening the doors. "Ḥophni! Pinḥas!" they called out in booming voices. And their shouts brought not only Eli's sons but Eli himself, leaning on Samuel's shoulder, to learn what the matter was.

As Eli heard what the messengers wished, his face darkened. "Is it the ark you want, indeed? Who told your elders and chieftains that the Almighty would agree? You think the ark will protect *you?* It is for us to protect the ark. How can you keep it safe, fighting an enemy for your very lives? And if any harm comes to it on your journey or in battle, how would you pay for the great sin? Leave the ark here, where it belongs. The Almighty can fight for you just as fiercely without it. Go, and tell your chieftains what I have said."

"Oh, father," said Ḥophni, "why do we need to worry so? With the ark they are sure to win. Stand aside, and Pinḥas and I will get it. And we will go with it to the battlefield. Think of it: we are sure to become heroes in the fighting."

"What?" cried Eli. "You would enter the chamber of the ark? That room is the Holy of Holies. Unless the entire *mishkan* must be moved, only the *kohen gadol* may enter—and only on *yom kippur,* the Day of Atonement. As long as I live, neither of you is yet the *kohen gadol!*"

"Oh, father," answered Ḥophni, "what does it matter? They *need* the ark. Who cares about the old laws?" And without a word Ḥophni and Pinḥas took two soldiers with them into the chambers of the *mishkan.* On the sides of the ark were rings that held two strong poles. By these poles the four lifted it and carried it out.

In Eli's face was a determination that his sons had never seen before. "Go, my sons," he said, "and do not return. Even if you live through the next battle, do not come before me ever again!" His sons grew pale, and they smiled no more.

Those with the keenest eyes in the Hebrew army saw it first—the ark of the covenant of the Almighty, whose spirit dwelt between the cherubim on top—as the gold flashed and gleamed in the sun. Soon all saw it, and everyone knew it had come to the camp. By the thousands they all gave a great shout that was both a battle-cry and a sound of joy. So great was their outburst that the very earth seemed to thunder in tumult, and it carried clearly to the Philistine camps in Aphek.

"What was that?" the Philistine soldiers asked one another. "What was that terrible shout in the Hebrew camp?" Frightened and uncertain, they sent spies to steal past the Hebrew guards and learn what had happened. Under the cover of nightfall the spies returned to their camp. And they told of the ark that was sacred to the Lord of the Hebrews—that it was in the other camp, and the entire army of Israel was now certain of victory.

The Philistines were frightened. "God Himself has come into their camp!" they cried. "Woe is us! Never before has anything like this happened. O, woe is us!

Who will save us from such divine powers? These are the powers that smote the Egyptians with every plague and affliction, even at the Red Sea in the wilderness."

But there were scornful men among the Philistines who laughed in derision even at the Almighty, the Lord of Israel. "What are you afraid of?" they cried to their fellow-soldiers. "The Lord of Israel had it in His power to bring ten plagues. Well, He brought them upon the Egyptians. Whatever else He could do, He did to the Egyptians at the Red Sea. He does not have a single plague left to bring upon us!"

"Wait and see," whispered a heavenly echo too faint for them to hear. "As you live! I shall bring upon you a plague that has never yet been seen, that has never yet existed in the world." But the Philistine soldiers heard nothing; and soon all were asleep in the dark.

Sharp at daybreak, before his men could give way to fear again, the Philistine commander called his troops swiftly into battle formation. Then he spoke aloud: "Be strong and act as men, O Philistines—or you will become slaves to the Hebrews as they have been slaves to you. Then be men, and fight!"

Overcoming their fear of the ark, the Philistines took courage. Once more the battle trumpets sounded, and chariots and lancers moved forward across the plain in a great mass of armor. And the Hebrews found, to their misfortune, that the ark would not help them. Had they turned to the Almighty Himself, to ask how they might win His help, victory might have been theirs. But now, as the sun rose high over the bloody day, Israel was badly defeated. Thirty thousand Hebrew soldiers fell dead. The rest ran screaming, off to their homes for safety, in complete disorder.

To the end, Ḥophni and Pinḥas stayed with the ark, certain that it would protect them. But as his shadow fell across them, a Philistine giant named Goliath raised his great sword in his right hand and sent it slashing down, bringing a swift end to their lives. (This was the same Goliath whom a Hebrew boy named David would kill with a stone from his sling, many years later.) With his left hand the giant picked up the ark and marched off with it. The three boxes set one inside the other—gold, wood, and gold again—were heavy enough. With the tablets of sapphire inside, on which the Ten Commandments were written, it always took four strong men to lift the ark by the poles at its sides. Goliath, however, carried it in his left hand like a sack of feathers.

In a deserted part of the plain, far from the shouting and running men, Goliath sat down, happy as a child with a new toy, to look inside the ark and find out what made it so holy. It took him a while before he managed to get the triple doors open and take out the two tablets of sapphire. And there he sat, admiring and wondering at the strange (Hebrew) letters he could not read.

In the town of Shiloh, not a sound of the fighting was heard. The battle raged some forty miles away, and neither the shouts of victory nor the cries of defeat traveled that far. In the hours after the army messengers had left with Ḥophni and Pinḥas, taking along the ark, all was silence.

From the courtyard of the *mishkan* Samuel moved Eli's great chair onto a little rock platform, not far from the town gate, that overlooked the vineyards and farms all about. Close by ran the road that led from the distant mountains through Shiloh. And in the chair Eli sat hour after hour, as the sun's position in the sky moved slowly toward the west. He was ninety-eight years old. His hair and beard had long ago turned the purest white; and he could no longer see at all. But weak and feeble as he was, he could not rest in his room. His heart was too full of worry, trembling for the ark. He feared it would never come back to the *mishkan* in Shiloh. So he sat on alone in the chair, with only Samuel coming every once in a while to attend to his needs. He waited for a runner to come from the battlefield, to bring him news.

In the town there were only old men now, and women and children. The younger men had all gone days before to join the Hebrew army. Early in the morning sun, as the children began to play, the older people learned how the ark had been taken away to the battlefield, as one person told another. And a lad named Saul, of the tribe of Benjamin, heard it too.

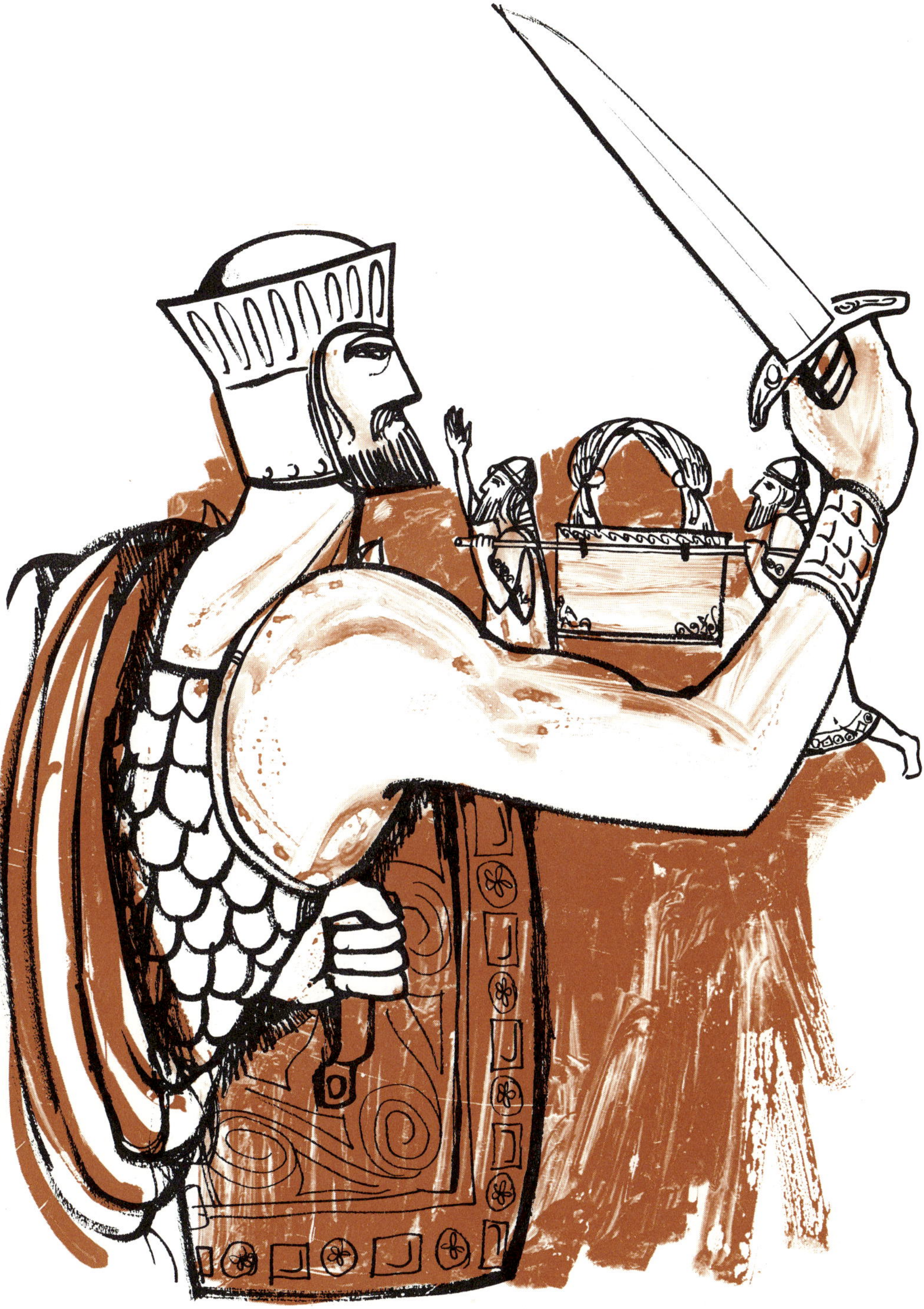

In all Shiloh there was no one, man or boy, who could run as fast as Saul. Suddenly he had an overwhelming desire to know what would become of the ark. Silently he set off on his lightning-swift feet, sped past Eli in his chair on the rock, and soon was lost from sight in the mountains. In a little while he reached the battlefield.

Once there, the lad did not stop. Between soldiers, horses and chariots young Saul ran swiftly on the battlefield, looking for the ark. He needed all his deftness and speed to keep clear of the Philistine swords and lances and spears. At last he caught sight of the giant Goliath carrying off the ark in one hand to a quiet, deserted part of the plain. Keeping well out of sight, young Saul followed on silent feet. And still as a mouse, he watched from behind a tree as Goliath worked the ark doors open and took out the tablets of the Ten Commandments.

The boy knew he could never fight the huge and mighty Goliath. But he trusted to his skillful feet. As the giant looked at the sapphire tablets in wonder, Saul moved like a flash. With two hands he yanked the tablets out of the giant's hold; and before the startled Goliath could realize what had happened, the boy was away, swift as a deer.

Goliath shrugged his shoulders. He saw it would be hopeless to chase the boy; he could never catch him. But at least he still had the ark itself, with the two cherubim, so finely made, on top. It was a splendid war prize,

Goliath thought, as he picked it up once more and began trudging back to the Philistine camp.

Meanwhile, Saul's agile feet took him quickly back through the afternoon to the town of Shiloh. Only after he finished his journey would he realize that something miraculous happened: Sapphire stone is extremely heavy, yet the two tablets sat on his shoulders as light as the wind.

On he ran, then, through the mountains and valleys. Only once did he stop—when it suddenly dawned on him that he had seen a great tragedy for his people on the battlefield. So many lay dead, and the rest were running away. The Hebrews had been badly defeated.

The boy stopped, and grief and sorrow filled his heart. He knew what people did when they grieved and mourned because someone in their family died. Now Saul did the same: he made a great tear in his clothes and smeared earth on his head. Then he picked up the two tablets and ran on to Shiloh.

In the town, the old men and the womenfolk tried to keep busy with daily chores and duties. But as the sun in the western sky cast its golden sheen over the flat roofs and white walls of their little houses, they kept looking out to the road from the mountains, waiting silently for some messenger to bring them news. For when they knew how the battle went, they would know if their own lives were safe. Should the Hebrew army fall, the Philistines would take more and more of their land, making slaves of all the people they conquered.

When the shadows of late afternoon grew long, they saw the boy, far off on the mountain road. In silence they gathered at the town gate to hear what news he would bring.

Saul stopped in their midst and waited to catch his breath. Then he told them all he had seen. And a great cry of woe rose from them. The worst of their fears had come true. Soon the Philistines would be in Shiloh too.

In his chair on the rocky platform, Eli heard the grieving outcry. "What is that uproar?" he asked in fright. Samuel, at his side, was about to reply, when Saul looked up from the town gate and saw the aged *kohen gadol*. Leaving the woe-stricken people behind him, the boy sped to Eli. "And who is this," asked the aged man, "who has now come running here? I have heard you, but I cannot see you. Do you know perhaps why some large crowd was making a tumult just now?"

"It was the news I brought from the battlefield," answered Saul. "Today I escaped from that battle and ran back here." And calmly Eli asked, "How did it go there, my son? Tell me everything that happened."

"Israel has fled in rout and disorder before the Philistines," said the boy; "and a great havoc and slaughter has befallen the people. And your two sons, Ḥophni and Pinḥas, are slain—and the ark of God was captured!"

As Saul told of the death of his sons, Eli's body

shook with a mighty tremor. But when he heard about the ark, a great moan escaped him: "What catastrophe is this?" he asked Samuel. "Your father brought me the prophecy that my two sons would die in one day. But neither you nor your father said anything about the ark! O, woe is me . . ." So violently did he shake and quiver that he fell backward out of the chair, to strike the edge of the platform of rock and roll down, until he lay close to the town gate.

Swiftly Samuel ran to help him. But as he looked at his aged master, Samuel knew there was nothing further he could do. Eli was dead.

In Samuel's head still rang the answer he had wanted to give to the *kohen gadol's* last, bitter outcry. He remembered the very first words of prophecy he had heard from the Almighty: "Behold, I am about to do something in Israel so dreadful that whoever hears it, his two ears shall tingle." For a long time now, Samuel had known that it meant an enemy would capture the holy ark. The Almighty had given His warning. But it was too late to tell this to Eli.

For forty years the *kohen gadol* had been a true and fair judge to his people. A good leader, he listened to their troubles and complaints, and always gave them good advice. Whenever two had an argument, he listened to both of them patiently, then settled their argument peacefully.

Now he lay dead near the town gate, broken by the

tragic news he had heard. There was nothing left to do but to bury him with great honor.

But still more tragedy was in store for Eli's family. In a house nearby, the wife of Eli's son Pinḥas lay in bed, about to give birth to a child. Soon enough she also learned the terrible news—just as her child was born. For her too the news was more than she could bear. Her husband was dead; her father-in-law was dead; and the people were defeated. Grief and despair came to claim her life too.

As she was breathing her last, the wife of Pinḥas looked with tear-filled eyes at her new-born son. "Let your name be *ee-kavod*," she whispered, naming him with two Hebrew words that meant "no glory." "All glory is gone from Israel, for the ark of God has been taken!" (So the new-born's name in English has remained *Ichabod*.)

Sadly and quietly Samuel packed his belongings. Three days before the tragic day of battle, he had heard the Almighty's soft words: "Go and visit the village of Ramah, where your parents live; and there you too shall live." Now he understood how wise were the Almighty's words. With Eli gone, there was no hope of keeping the *mishkan* open. The Philistines might come at any time, and leave everything in ruins.

Taking others from the tribe of Levi to help him, Samuel buried the *menorah* and the many other holy objects of the *mishkan*, where no Philistine would ever find them. With them he also buried the two tablets of sapphire stone that the boy Saul had managed to bring back. Then he gave the people of Shiloh a firm order: They were to pack their things, gather their families, and move far inland. No one was to remain.

His last look at the little town was long and thoughtful. Then he was off.

Mounted on a sure-footed donkey, Samuel looked all about him. He had come to Shiloh as a little boy; he was leaving as a young man. He had come in a happier time, when his people lived in peace. He was leaving in a time of deep sadness for his people. He too would have given way to gloom and despair if he did not remember what else the Almighty said when He had told him to leave Shiloh and go to Ramah: "Yet in your lifetime, O Samuel, you will see the fate that I shall bring on My enemies. The Philistines shall perish and be destroyed by every kind of noisome creeping thing. Wait, and you will see!"

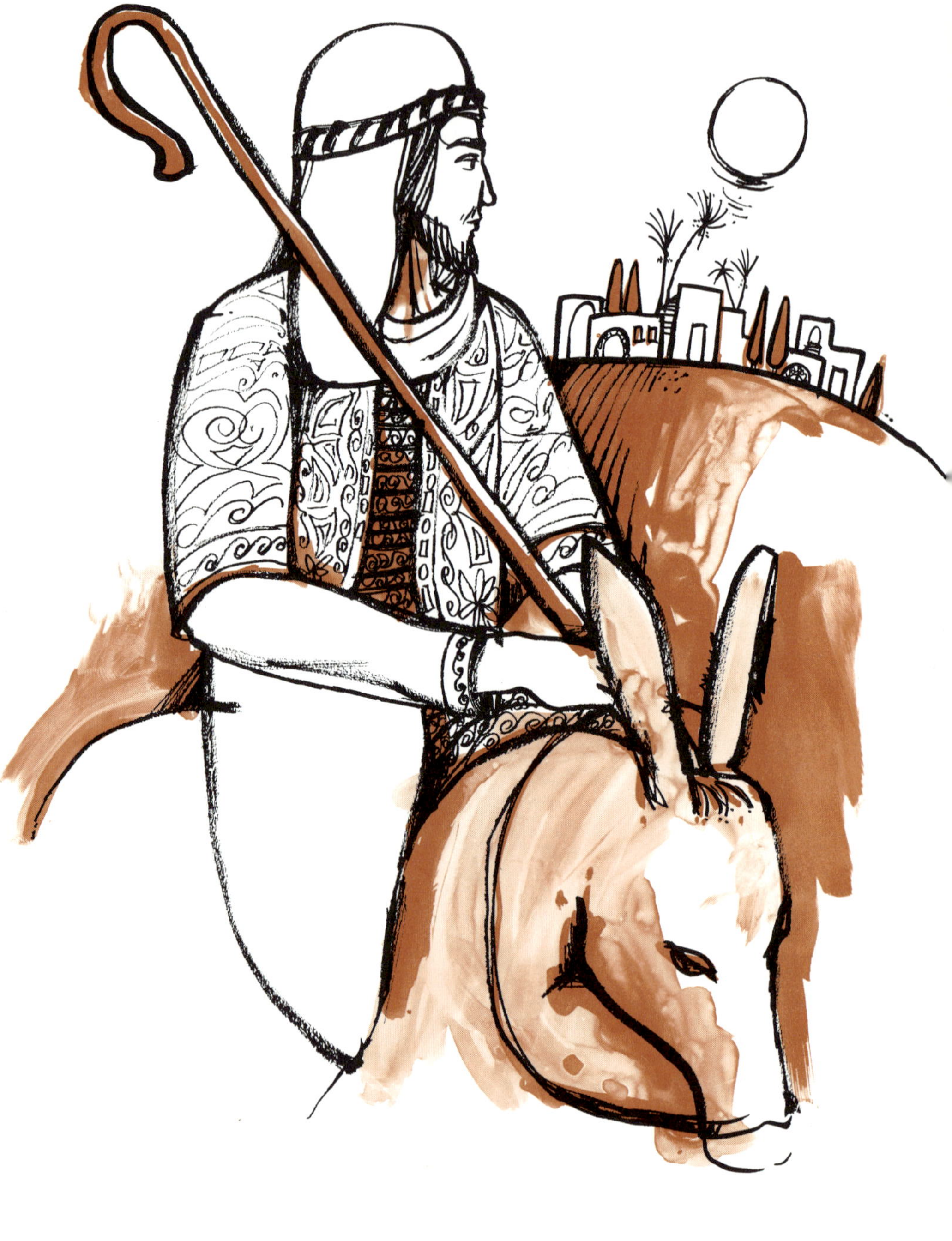

10

OF MICE AND A PLAGUE

The Philistines were weary of fighting. As they gathered back at their camp in Aphek, they thought only of going home to their five cities for a good rest. Then the news spread among them of the magnificent war-prize that the giant Goliath had captured—Israel's holy ark! And they whooped for joy.

Since Goliath lived in Ashdod, it was decided that out of the Philistines' five cities, Ashdod should have the honor of keeping this triple box with the golden cherubim on top. And without delay, they made ready for their procession of triumph.

The rulers of the five cities knew, however, that the ark was extremely holy: it was a kind of throne for the Almighty whom Israel worshipped—the Almighty who had brought such dreadful plagues on the Egyptians long ago. It would not be wise to let the Philistine soldiers see it directly with their eyes, or great harm might befall them. So the five rulers covered the ark with a thick cloth, which they tied fast. Then the procession began.

At the head went Goliath, the covered ark resting lightly on his back. Then came the thousands of soldiers, singing and shouting. Not since the day Samson had been brought captive to their city of Gaza had the Philistines celebrated with such frenzy. Far into the night the revelry continued.

In the royal palace of Ashdod the five rulers met again, to consider. "Well," asked one of them, "where shall we keep this ark?" And another replied: "We have our idol Dagon, that we worship; and it stands in its own temple. This ark is also an idol, that Israel worships. It is just as holy to the Hebrews as the idol of Dagon is to us. Well then, let us put the ark in the same temple, right next to Dagon. Thus we will treat it with full honor, and the God of the Hebrews will not be angry with us."

Near the five rulers sat the priests who served in the temple of Dagon; and they did not like his plan at all. To them the idol of Dagon, a huge statue that looked like a man from the waist up and like a fish from the waist down, represented the greatest god in the world. They wanted no other idol set alongside their Dagon as though it were equally great.

"My lords and masters," said the head priest, "I think this worthy plan can be improved. After all, our army defeated the Hebrews splendidly. That means that Dagon is greater than any Divine Being in whom they believe. Then let us put this ark in our temple, but *not* alongside Dagon. Let us rather put it *before* Dagon, at his feet — to show that the weaker idol must serve the victorious one."

This plan seemed fine and wise, and all agreed. On the floor of the magnificent temple, facing Dagon's tremendous feet, the priests set down the ark, and removed the cover. Round and about they danced and shouted, in a celebration of their own.

But night's darkness brought an end to all the happiness and excitement in Ashdod. The thousands of victorious Philistines went off to find places to sleep. The priests of Dagon shut the great temple doors of brass, and went to their homes. Nearby, the waves of the sea slapped and broke on the shore in a distant lullaby, as the silent moon looked on.

Bright and early the next morning, the people of Ashdod came thronging to the temple of Dagon, as the smiling priests grandly opened the great doors. All were eager to see the captured Hebrew idol. Dagon was indeed mighty, they thought, to make their fighting men so strong in battle. All of Canaan used to worship Dagon as the god that made the grain grow well in the fields (*dagan* is the word for grain in Hebrew). The people of Ashdod were proud of their idol.

But what in the world was this? Across the whole floor of the temple lay the great statue; it had fallen face downward before the holy ark, which stood untouched in its place.

"What happened?" asked the excited people. "It

looks as if Dagon is bowing to the Hebrew ark! How did it happen?"

"It is nothing—nothing at all," answered the priests smoothly, their smiles still on their faces. "There must have been a small tremor, a light little earthquake during the night, too small for us to notice, and it made Dagon fall. It was only an accident . . . only an accident. We will put Dagon back in place now, and you can come again in the afternoon. Go home now, and come back later. All will be well!"

It took the strength of many men, as they pulled and heaved with their thick ropes, to lift the idol back in place. But at last Dagon was set upright, looking as majestic as ever. And in the afternoon the crowds of people came to enjoy the sight. From near and far they came, joking and laughing at their triumph over the Hebrews—until night fell and it was time for the priests to shut the temple's brass doors. The priests also smiled and joked, still feeling proud—so proud, in fact, that they did not hear a heavenly echo whisper, "You learned nothing from a lukewarm lesson. Then you will learn from a lesson of boiling heat."

The next morning, once more with grinning faces, the priests proudly opened the temple doors to the people of Ashdod. Then the grins and smiles suddenly vanished, and they moved to quickly shut the doors again.

"What is the matter?" asked the people in front, who had been about to enter. "What happened? Was that Dagon on the floor? Has he fallen again? And was that his hand we saw, cut off like that?"

"It is nothing," said the priests, now pale and trembling, "nothing at all—just another accident. We will have to close the temple again, for a few weeks, perhaps—until we can make a few repairs. Have no fear!"

Yet the priests were plainly frightened themselves, as they sent the people home. For in the temple, the statue of Dagon had fallen again on its face before the Hebrew ark—and this time no one could believe that a tiny earthquake had toppled it. The idol's head and two hands had somehow been cut cleanly off and left neatly on the threshold of the temple. (Thus the threshold became sacred to the priests; and never again did a priest of Dagon step on the threshold of his temple; it had to be jumped over.)

How dearly the priests wanted to keep the new disaster a secret. But they could not. The next few months, they had to keep the temple closed, while they worked away to repair the statue and set it aright. And in those months, the trouble that had befallen Dagon became known to all.

(In those months the Philistine soldiers also marched forth again, to seize more of Israel's defenseless territory. They occupied the hill country, and left their garrisons to keep control. To the town of Shiloh, where they found not a soul, they set fire; and the *mishkan* went up in flames, never to be rebuilt there. Having taken the central part of the land, the Philistine soldiers left their garrisons in charge, and returned to their five cities.)

At last Dagon stood upright again in the temple of Ashdod, as good as new. The priests wondered if it would be wise to leave the ark where it was and simply open the temple doors to the people once more. Then a new disaster struck, and they forgot their thoughts entirely.

Here, there, everywhere, the mice appeared: in the nooks and crannies of the city's homes, in the fields and vineyards of neighboring villages, in barns and cellars and attics. Everywhere the little scurrying creatures gnawed and ate their way, ruining food and crops and property. And with them came vermin, horrid little insects, bringing the dread contagious disease of bubonic plague. Through all of Ashdod and its nearby villages, people became feverish, and swellings appeared in the hidden parts of their bodies—swellings that turned into bleedings boils. One after another, people began to die.

In the city of Ashdod there were too many dead to bury at once. The living piled the bodies in heaps; then they went to the palace of their *seren*, the ruler. And they shouted: "Let the ark of the God of Israel not stay here, with us. For His hand is punishing us heavily, together with our god Dagon. Send the ark away, or we will die!"

The *seren* of Ashdod acted swiftly. First he summoned the temple priests. "Well," he barked, "do you still think your plan was good? You would not let us set the ark side by side with Dagon. You had to put it opposite Dagon, at his feet, to show that our god was triumphant. And now the people are dying. You deserve at least the same fate."

Palace guards brought the priests to the hanging-place, where criminals were always put to death. There the angry people gathered and hanged every one of the priests of Dagon.

But the *seren* of Ashdod knew there was more to do. His messengers rode swiftly to the four other cities of the Philistines and brought back their rulers and high officers. In the royal palace they sat, as the *seren* of Ashdod asked, "What shall we do with the ark of the God of Israel? I tell you, I will not have it in Ashdod another day. Since it has come, it has brought nothing but trouble. Our idol of Dagon lies broken, and the people pile their dead in heaps." He told them of the plague that had struck Ashdod.

"Why are you so frightened?" asked the *seren* of Gath. "Have you forgotten how soundly we defeated the Hebrews at Eben-ezer? Come with me to the battlefield, and I will show you their dead still lying there, not buried. I tell you, Dagon is mightier than the Ruler of Israel. If your idol fell and broke, it was an accident. I am not afraid. I say we keep the ark."

"Keep it then," said the *seren* of Ashdod, "but not in my city."

The ruler of Gath spoke with his officers in whispers for a moment. Then he said, "It is our plan that the ark should make the rounds from one city to another, to stay in each city for a little while. In that way we shall all share in celebrating its capture. And if there is any danger, we will all share in that too. I propose that it be taken first to Gath."

The mice and the bubonic plague could travel just as fast as the holy ark (if not faster). No sooner was the ark in Gath than its people knew the same misery and woe as the Philistines of Ashdod. Panic seized the city as young and old began dying off. And the cry arose also in Gath, "Send away the ark! Let us be rid of it!"

Still the Philistine rulers would not yield to fear, and the ark was simply taken to Ekron, the next of their five cities. The *seren* of Ekron told his people nothing about any illness or plague; but the riders of Gath talked readily. Having brought the ark by wagon, they met some of the townspeople of Ekron, and told of all that had happened in Ashdod and Gath.

As the word spread with the speed of lightning, the people gathered before the *seren's* palace. "Now they have brought it around to us," they cried, "this ark of the God of Israel. Do they want to kill us and all our people?" The *seren* looked out and saw the fury of the mob. But he ruled with an iron hand, and would let no

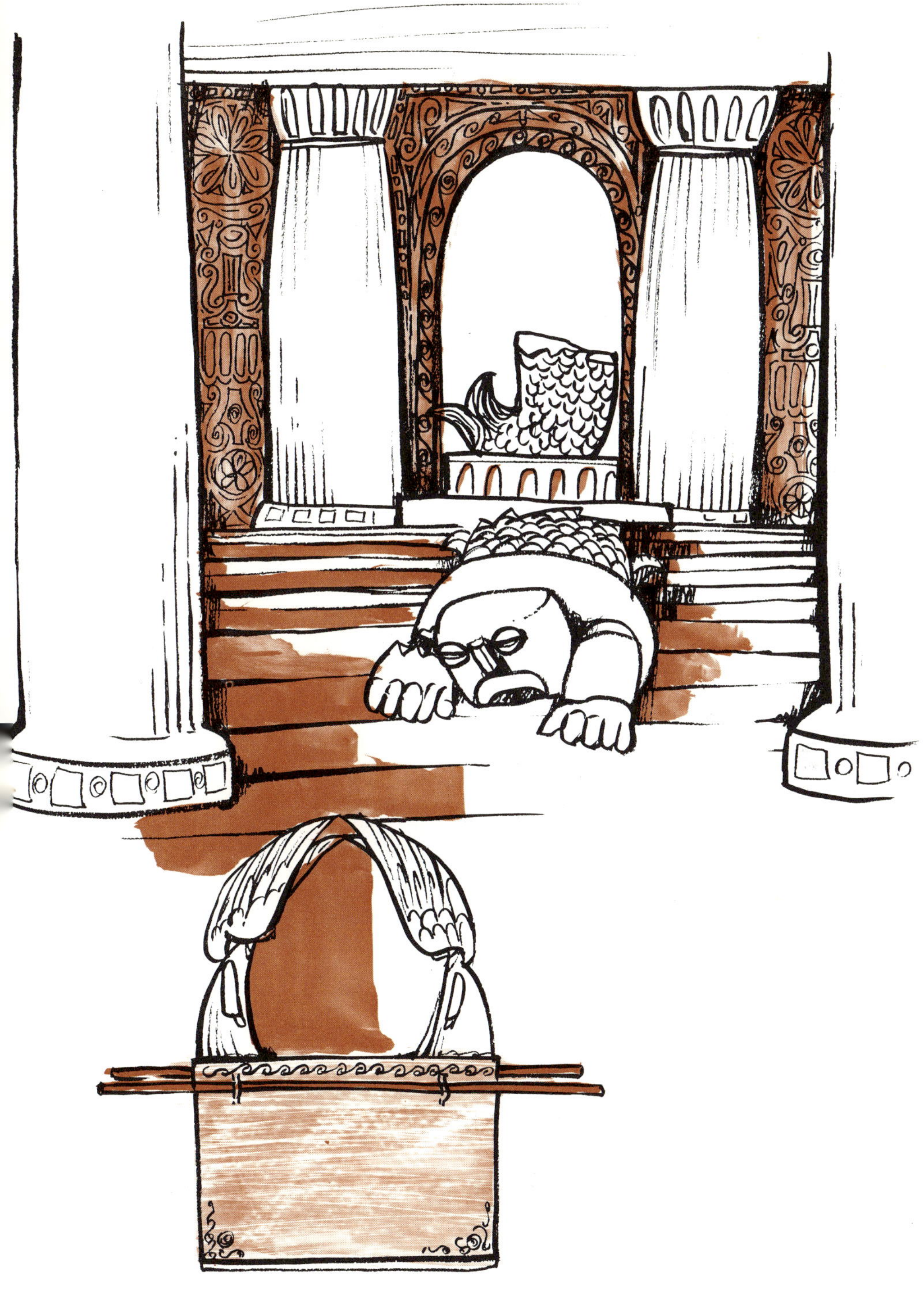

mob give him orders. His palace guards forced the people away to their homes, and then they put the ark in Ekron's temple.

The next day, however, the *seren* of Ekron sent his swiftest couriers to bring the other four rulers with all possible speed. For the bubonic plague and the swarms of rodents that came to Ekron were far worse than what Ashdod and Gath had suffered. And when the five rulers were all there, none spoke any longer with pride or bravado. They knew that in the three cities hardly a healthy man was yet alive: whoever was still living, was dreadfully ill.

One *seren* remembered suddenly what some of his fiercest soldiers had said when the Israelites had brought the ark to their camp. Many Philistine soldiers had become terrified then; but his strong fighters had shouted, "There is nothing to fear about the God of the Hebrews. He had ten plagues to hurl down, and He used them up on the Egyptians. He has no plagues left for us!"

As the *seren* remembered, he heartily wished that his fearless fighters might have kept their mouths closed.

11

THE ARK RETURNS

It was seven months since the Philistines had captured the ark and brought it to their territory. Now the five rulers sat in silent misery, until the *seren* of Ekron muttered, "Send away that ark of the God of Israel. Let it go back where it belongs, so that it will not kill us and our people."

"We certainly all agree," said another, "that this is what we must do. But how? How do we send it? And *where* do we send it? The Hebrew no longer have their holy place in Shiloh." And as none had any answer, the rulers sent for their high priests and seers. "What shall we do with the ark of the Lord?" they asked. "Tell us: how can we send it to its proper place, so that the God of the Hebrews will end His anger and His terrible punishment?"

For a short while the priests and seers spoke among themselves in whispers and murmurs. "Well, now," came their answer, "if you mean to send back the ark of the God of Israel, you must not send it just by itself, without a gift. You must send back an offering to Him, for the wrong you have done to His holiness. Then you will be healed from all this illness—since we can tell you beyond any doubt that *He* has brought these calamities which now afflict us — for then there will be no reason why His punishing hand should not leave you and turn back."

For a moment there was silence. "Now then," continued the spokesman for the priests and seers, "what offering shall we send back to Him for our wrong? ... Five golden ornaments in the shape of boils (the boils and sores that have afflicted our people), and five mice of gold — for you rulers of the Philistines are five in number, and one and the same plague has come for all the cities and all the rulers. So you must make golden images of your ills and of the creatures that are ravaging and destroying the land; and thus you will pay honor to the God of Israel, admitting that you have sinned against Him. Then He will surely lighten His hand and lift His punishment from you, your god, and your land."

"I must say," snapped the *seren* of Gath, "you give away our gold quite freely. Why must we send all that gold? Is it then so absolutely certain that the God of the Hebrews brought these troubles upon us, because of His ark? Has plague never struck any other land? Have rodents never invaded any other country? Do other people live in constant sunshine and peace because they have *not* taken the ark? What makes you so sure of what we must do? Perhaps these dreadful things will soon go away of themselves."

"O lords and masters," cried the spokesman for the priests and seers, "why should you harden your hearts and turn stubborn, just as the Egyptians and their Pharaoh hardened their hearts centuries ago? They would not let His people go freely to worship Him. And do you not know that in the end, when He made sport of them with His plagues, they let the people go, and out they went?"

In the meeting room all was silence. None of the Philistine rulers dared say another word. "Very well," grunted the *seren* of Gath.

"Now then," the spokesman continued. "Take the finest materials and make a new cart; get two milk cows which have never had a yoke put on them to pull a plow; and you must harness the cows to the cart, while you bring their young calves back to their barn, away from them. Then you shall take the ark of the Lord and put it in the cart. The golden figures which you are sending along as an offering to pay for your wrong, you will place in a little casket, a box at its side. Then send it off, and let it go."

The Philistine rulers considered the plan very thoughtfully.

"Do you understand what we are proposing?" asked the spokesman for the priests and seers. "You will take cows that have never borne a yoke to pull a plow. We should not expect them to want to pull the cart all by themselves. Furthermore, they will be cows that have given birth to calves a little while before, and are still caring for their young. When you take the calves away from them and put them back in the barn, we shall expect the cows to turn right around and go to their young." The five rulers nodded their heads in complete agreement.

"This, then," said the spokesman, "is the test. You will watch: If they take the ark up by way of His country's border, to Beth-shemesh, then you will be sure that He has done this deep harm to us. If they do not take the ark, then we shall know that not His hand touched us with this affliction, but it happened to us by chance."

The five rulers were agreed: the plan was excellent. They set their finest goldsmiths to work to fashion five images of boils and sores, and five golden mice. Using the best wood, skilled craftsmen prepared a superb cart with large solid wheels. Two cows were found exactly as the Philistine priests wanted. And when all was ready, the priests lifted the ark carefully by the poles in its side rings, and set it neatly in the cart. To the side of the ark they attached a little casket, a wooden chest of exquisite workmanship, that already contained the ten golden ornaments and objects, all securely wrapped. Over the ark they now placed a cloth of embroidered linen to cover it completely, cherubim and all. After all that had happened, they would not risk letting their people look directly at the ark any more: it could well bring more harm.

The morning was clear and lovely, for it was the harvest season. All about stood the people of Ekron, gathered to watch these strange preparations. They had been given the strictest orders that no one was to touch or guide or call the two cows which were now being harnessed to the cart, while their young calves were locked inside a barn close by. The people watched in silence.

For a moment the cows stood still, as no human hand touched or held them any longer. Then, of a sudden, they strained together against the harness, until the large heavy cartwheels turned; and they moved slowly on. Through the city's early morning shadows they went, until they were past the gate and into the bright warmth of the sun. Before them stretched the main road, to the next Philistine city. Another road branched off from it to lead to nearby farms and villages. Yet moving together, the animals turned southheast across a wild, unsettled plain, toward the valley of Sorek. No path was marked on that plain, yet they went along an exact line, straight toward Beth-shemesh, the Hebrew town that lay closest to the Philistines. Across the trackless plain the cows seemed to see a highway, which they followed steadily, although they lowed and mooed with yearning for their calves. They turned neither right nor left from their course. Behind them walked the five Philistine rulers, following and watching in silent wonder.

And it is told that as the two animals walked, they

turned their heads back to face the ark; and the air was filled with song—song which, to the astounded Philistine rulers who followed, seemed to come from the cows:

Arise, O ark of acacia wood,
and onward soar in splendor and might;
adorned in gold, you ever stood
in His holiest palace, in glorious light,
cherubim gleaming — a radiant sight!

To the very border of Beth-shemesh the five Philistine rulers followed the cart, convinced now past any doubt that all their troubles had come from the Almighty, whom the Hebrews worshipped.

It was harvest time, and the people of Beth-shemesh were in their fields to cut and gather the ripe wheat in their valley. The sun poured down its bright heat without mercy, and soon the workers found their clothes unbearable. At an early hour they removed their outer garments and left them lying at the edges of their fields.

From a hill high above the valley, the Philistine rulers watched in silence, while the cows continued on their way. "Come," said one of them. "We have just paid great honor to their God by sending back the ark in that manner. Now let us sneak down and gather their clothes, and we will leave them hidden somewhere about. Then we will see how much respect and honor *they* show Him when the ark reaches them."

No sooner said than done. From afar the five were

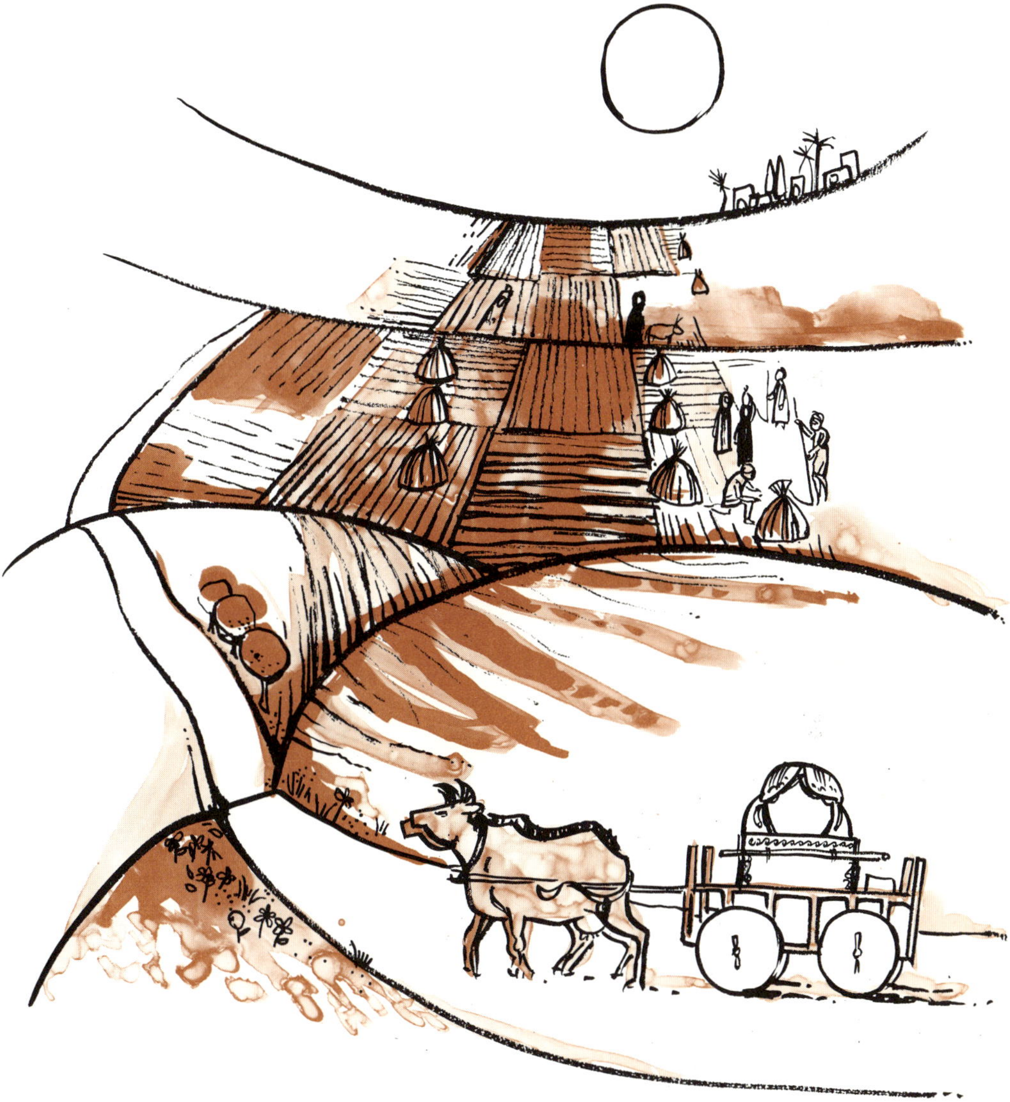

well-nigh invisible as they slid down to the valley in almost perfect silence. And the tall grasses hardly stirred as they went from one place to another swiftly gathering the Hebrews' garments. The five put all the clothing on the branches of a thick tree whose wide-spreading leaves let nothing be seen. Then, as silently as they had come, the five went back to the top of the hill, to continue watching. And the people in the fields saw nothing and suspected nothing.

On went the cows without a pause until they reached the fields in the valley. As they drew the cart in view of the Hebrew reapers, a sudden gust of wind blew away the embroidered linen that had covered the ark. The Hebrews looked up, and their eyes opened wide. "See that!" they marvelled. "There was not a man leading these cows, and they brought the ark back to us."

But the great holiness of the ark meant nothing to them. Seeing it exposed, with nothing to cover it, they should have bowed down to the ground until a cloth could be wrapped about it once more. Insted, they simply kept staring at it, grinning foolishly — not even turning their heads away. Nor did anyone even think to look for the clothes they had laid aside, that they might appear before it more respectfully.

Now some merely went up to the ark and asked, "Who annoyed you until you became angry with us and left? And who made you calm and cheerful so that you became friendly to us and returned?" Then others, trying to keep on with their harvesting, began to cut wheat and bow down, cut wheat and bow down — making a funny kind of dance.

As the cows continued pulling the cart, the people took to following it in their high spirits, jumping, dancing, doing handstands, and making all kinds of jokes. And at last, too curious to hold back any longer, they opened the doors of the ark to peer inside. The tablets of stone were not there, since Goliath the Philistine giant had taken them out months before; but they saw the rolled-up scroll of the Torah which Moses had himself written for his people in the wilderness.

The cows brought the cart to the field of a farmer named Joshua, and there they stopped close to a huge stone; not another step would they take. Many more workers could see the ark now, as the wings of the golden cherubim blazed in the sun; and they came running to join the others. Among them were members of the tribe of Levi, who remembered what they had been taught. Bidding the Israelites bow down and keep their eyes closed, they carefully lifted the ark off the cart and set in on the large stone. They noticed the beautiful wooden box attached to the side. In silence they took it off and put it on the ground nearby. Later they would see what it contained. Now they brought a large heavy cloth and covered the ark securely. With a shout of joy the Israelites rose from the ground, and they began their celebration for the ark that had returned.

Since the cows and the cart had brought the ark, the men of the tribe of Levi knew they were holy now, and might not be used for anything else. The people broke up the cart and split the wood into pieces, which they piled on a *bamah,* a high platform of earth that could serve as an altar. With the wood blazing away, they offered sacrifices. (Now that the *mishkan* was no more, a *kohen* was not needed; any Israelite might offer sacrifice on *a bamah.*)

The happiness of the people knew no bounds. They sent off messengers to every nearby town and city to spread the news. From near and far the Israelites came to see for themselves the ark that had come back by a miracle. And the people brought their own animals to offer as sacrifices near the ark. With the meat of their offerings they made great feasts for all their neighbors and friends. That entire day, the countryside rang with the sounds of their happiness.

Meanwhile, the men of the tribe of Levi (the Levites) opened the wooden chest. When they found the five golden ornaments shaped like boils and sores, the eldest Levite understood at once, and he explained to the others: The Philistines had been stricken with bubonic plague, and they sent the five ornaments for their five large cities, as an offering to the God of the Hebrews, that He should forgive them for taking the ark.

Then the Levites found the golden creatures—five large ones, and dozens of smaller ones. "I think," said the eldest with a smile, "that every Philistine town and village must have prepared a little ornament for itself to go into this chest, in addition to the five large ones for the big cities—to make sure that our Lord would keep them safe from the plagues."

"Well," asked another Levite, "what are we to do with all these objects?"

"We must keep them safe," answered the eldest, "until the time comes to build a new House for the Almighty. Then these will be melted down and the gold can be used. For they are the property of the Almighty."

As the Israelites learned what precious ornaments the Philistines had sent, and why they had sent them, they had even more reason to celebrate. Powerful indeed was the Divine Ruler whom they worshipped. And so the celebration continued without pause, until the setting sun, painting the sky in deep purples and reds, reminded them that night was coming. They began to separate to leave, some to go home, some to spend the night in the pleasant fields.

It was then that they found people lying dead here and there in the field of Joshua the farmer. Their laughter ended, and in shocked silence they gathered the bodies before the covered ark. There were seventy bodies in all: Seventy who had been alive to celebrate during the day, were no longer living.

High above in the mountains, five pairs of keen eyes stopped watching, and the five Philistine rulers grunted with satisfaction. They had recognized the seventy dead: those were the reapers and farmers who had first seen the ark, as soon as it reached Beth-shemesh — and they had treated it without any respect or honor. The Almighty did not forget, and as the day wore on, they fell lifeless one by one. Now the Philistine rulers knew that the ark brought punishment to *anyone* who treated it wrongly: The Almighty of Israel punished Philistine and Hebrew alike.

In the dusk that fell between day and night, the five rulers went back to their land.

But in Beth-shemesh no one knew why these seventy had died. The Hebrews could only think that the ark had somehow been the cause—and a great wailing and woe-crying arose. As the news of the tragedy spread, the shock and pain were as great as if not seventy but 50,000 had died. In the past few months the Philistines had slain their people by the thousands. Now, the cry arose, the ark was killing more. And the Hebrews all about moaned: If the ark brought death to these seventy, it could go on slaying more and more! When, where would death stop? "O, who can stand in the presence of the Lord, this God so sacred? We cannot take care of this ark, bewaring always of its holiness. To whom can it go up? Where can we send it, away from us?"

The people of Beth-shemesh sent couriers to far-off Kiryath Y'arim with a message: "The Philistines have returned the ark of the Lord. Come down and take it up to you." So men of the tribe of Levi came from far-off Kiryath Y'arim, nine miles west of Jerusalem, and they took up the ark. To a hill in their town they took it, bearing its poles on their shoulders, and they set it down in the house of a Levite named Abinadab. The man had a grown son named El'azar, who was pious by nature; and El'azar was put in charge. It would be his duty to keep the room where it stood clean and holy; and he was to keep all curious strangers away from it.

Twenty years were to pass before the ark left the house of Abinadab.

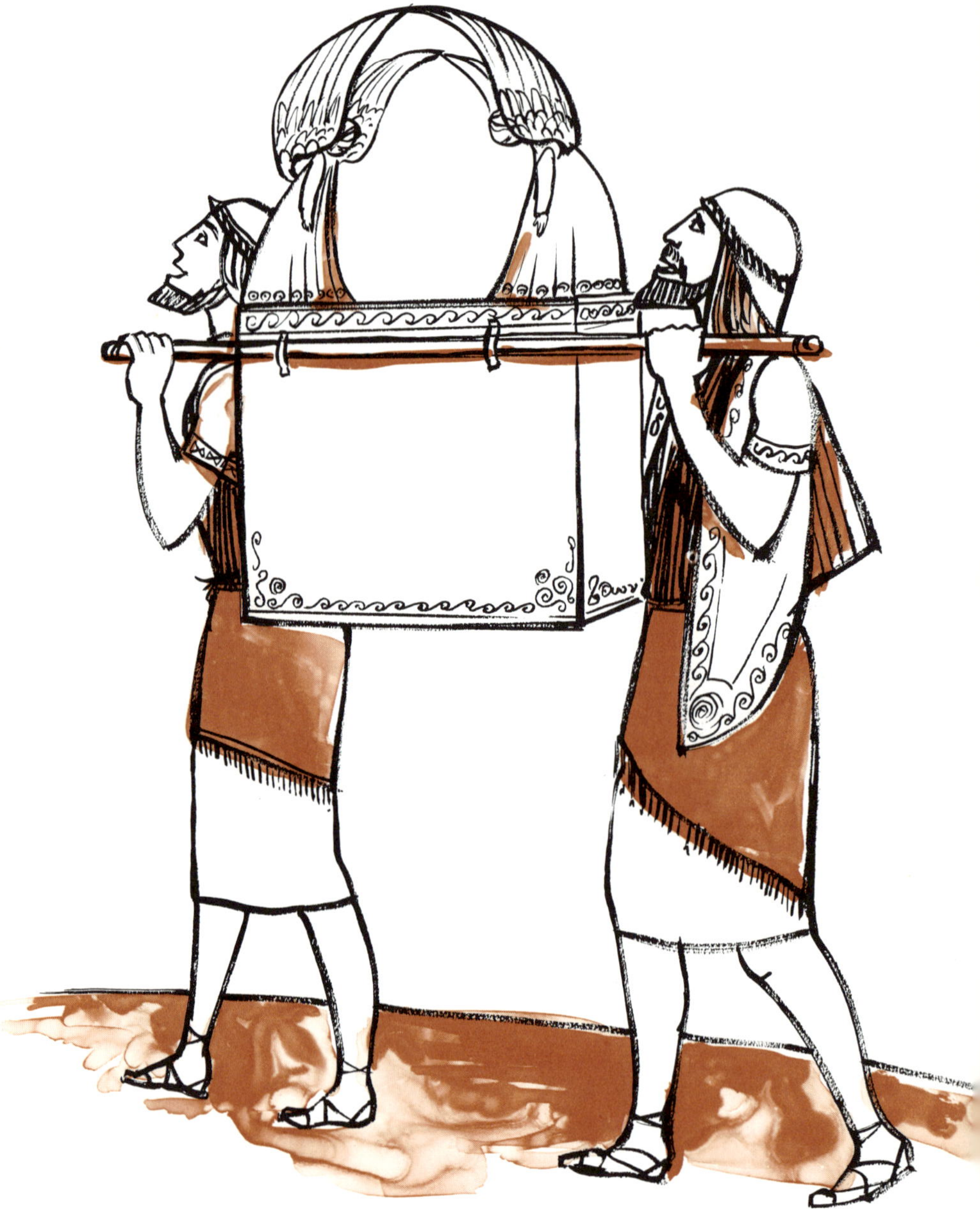

12

SAMUEL TAKES CHARGE

At his home in Ramah, Samuel led a serene, quiet life. But he knew what was happening with the people of Israel. He learned soon enough how the ark had come back; and then he was told of the seventy who had perished in Beth-shemesh the very day the ark returned there. By his prophetic powers he learned how they had sinned to deserve death.

Samuel was saddened. He knew there were many in the land who would have acted as wickedly and foolishly as the seventy in Beth-shemesh. For few people knew the Torah of the Almighty. Having captured the land of Canaan, the Hebrews became farmers, as the people of Canaan had been before them. And from the foreigners who remained among them, the Hebrews learned of the idols of Baal and Ashtoreth that Canaan used to worship, to make certain the crops would grow well on the land. Long ago the Hebrews had found such idols, left behind by the people of Canaan. Then, as the Torah was slowly forgotten, the Hebrews copied these idols of

Baal and Ashtoreth, and took to worshipping them so that *their* farms would grow food aplenty.

Samuel could no longer rest at home. Now that the ark had come back by a true miracle, the people were ready to listen and believe in the Almighty and His Torah. They needed only a good teacher. And Samuel knew that he alone must go and teach them now. For this his mother had promised him to the Almighty yet before he was born.

Samuel remembered how his father used to take a different route every time he went to Shiloh for a Festival, so as to reach many towns and villages and persuade the people there to come along. Now *he* would have to reach many towns and villages.

From Ramah, in the center of the tribe of Benjamin's territory, he set off for Bethel; and from Bethel he went to far-off Gilgal, east of Jericho; then on he went to Mizpah, five miles north of Jerusalem. All along the way he stopped at every village he found, and the people gathered to hear him. He spoke passionately, telling first of the plagues that had struck the Philistines, and of the miraculous way the ark had returned to the Hebrews. "Do you not see," he cried, "that the Philistines are no match for the power of the Almighty? For the sake of His ark, He made them suffer heavily. O my people, let *us* belong to the Almighty as much as the ark —let us worship Him and obey His commandments—and even so will He strike down the Philistines for *our* sake!"

Tears came to the eyes of his listeners. For all these months they were living in fear of the Philistines, wondering when this cruel enemy would come to their towns and villages, to murder them or make slaves of them. Now Samuel was telling them, with the certainty of absolute truth, that the Almighty could strike down this enemy for them: "Speak!" they exclaimed. "Tell us how we can become the Almighty's people. How shall we worship Him?'

"Would you turn to the Eternal Lord now with all your heart?"

"Yes!" they cried.

"Then get rid of the foreign gods among you. Throw out your idols of Baal and Ashtoreth, to which you bow down. And set your heart to the Lord alone, the Creator of heaven and earth who is everywhere, who cannot be pictured by any idol or statue. Worship and pray to Him alone, and He will make you safe from the Philistine power."

So Samuel spoke wherever he stopped on his travels, and people gathered to hear him. His listeners would offer him the finest gifts—food and drink, gold and silver, sheep and cattle. For it was the custom that whenever someone brought a message from a dream or a prophecy that comforted them, people rewarded him with gifts (and some made up messages that were completely untrue, merely for the sake of the gifts they would receive). Samuel refused to take anything. Wherever he went, his donkey carried along a tent and a supply of food. Until he returned to his home in Ramah, he slept in no one's house and ate at no one's table.

So Samuel's words spread far and wide, as the Hebrews learned that he spoke honestly, and not to gain wealth for himself. Everywhere they threw out and destroyed their idols of Baal and Ashtoreth.

Soon after he returned from his travels, Samuel set out again from Ramah. This time he sent messengers through all the land, with one message for his people: "Gather all Israel at Mizpah, and I will pray for you to the Lord." And straight to Mizpah, in the highlands of the tribe of Benjamin's territory, Samuel himself rode. For Mizpah was a holy place in Israel, where a permanent altar stood. There Joshua had received great help from Heaven in his battle for the land.

As Samuel stood at the altar and looked out, he could see faces like grass in the countryside, that seemed to reach the horizon. For the Hebrews had gathered in Mizpah by the thousands. In front were the elders; at a sign from Samuel they began to draw water from a nearby well, which they then spilled over the altar as an offering to the Almighty.

Samuel raised his hand. "As this water is poured out before the Lord," he cried, "let us pour our hearts out in prayer before Him. And as the water washes clean all it touches, so may we be cleansed and forgiven for all the wrongs we have done." The elders drew more water, which was passed among the Hebrews for all to drink. And it is told that those who had removed the idols of Baal and Ashtoreth from their homes and turned to the Almighty, were able to speak then as well as before. But those who had kept their idols, thinking it might be well to continue worshipping them, could not open their mouths now to utter a word. These sinful people Samuel took aside into a separate group, and he spoke long and earnestly to them—until at last most of them felt sick and sorry for their foolishness.

The entire day the Hebrews stayed in Mizpah, fasting; no food touched their mouths, as they confessed all their sins and bad deeds, asking the Almighty to forgive them and protect them.

That day Samuel also sat as a judge of his people. If anyone had a quarrel with his neighbor about a cow or a piece of land, the two came before the prophet. Samuel listened to their arguments, and decided which of the two was right. Hundreds came before him, and he listened patiently to them all, giving wise answers and decisions. Again, many offered him gifts—for it was the custom to reward a man with gifts if he acted as a judge over the quarrel of two people (and many a man acting as judge would therefore favor a rich man in an argument with a poor man, expecting a richer reward). But again Samuel took absolutely nothing from the people. He merely ended the quarrels and arguments among them, until the Hebrews felt united, as one people.

The Philistines, however, had not been idle. From their mountain-top their soldiers noticed the great gathering at Mizpah. A few stole down to get a closer look, then rode at top speed to their five fortified cities. To the Philistine rulers, so many Hebrews in one place meant but one thing: Israel must be preparing for war against them. Instantly each *seren* summoned the fighting men of his city; and together they began a rapid march on Mizpah, as the sun beat down on their red cloaks and plumed helmets.

It was not long before the Hebrews caught sight of their dreaded enemy swarming over the distant mountains toward them. For a moment they were silent with fear, as they watched the thousands of foot-soldiers, horses and chariots. Then a great lament arose to Samuel: "Do not be still now for us. Cry to the Lord our God, and let Him save us from the power of the Philistines!"

Samuel looked carefully at the distant mountains. It would be some time before the Philistine army reached his people. Calmly he took a young lamb and offered it as a sacrifice. Then he began to pray: "O Master of the world, what do You ask of a man?—only that he should say before You honestly, *I have done wrong*. The people of Israel now say before You, *We have done wrong*; will You not forgive them?" And Samuel knew the Almighty would answer.

He was still attending to his offering on the altar when the Philistine army came charging full speed across the fields toward the great gathering of Hebrews. In another few moments they could begin slashing with their swords and thrusting with their spears. Suddenly the earth under the Philistines quivered and shook, as an earthquake opened great tears and cracks in it. And overhead, thunder roared and lightning crackled and flashed. Many fell into the the earth's new cracks and openings; many more felt their faces scorched by the great sheets of fire and heat that blazed up from the cracked and broken earth. And the rest were frightened and confused. Their swift horses, on which they always relied to carry them and pull their chariots, no longer knew where to go. The terrified animals neighed and whinnied; rearing up on their hind legs, they went crashing and falling all about. And soon the Philistines were not one army any more. In their terror and pain they became scattered into little groups without leaders. They dropped their weapons and ran in every direction.

"After them!" cried Samuel. And with him in the lead, the Hebrews gave chase. Some picked up rocks and sticks; others soon found the swords, spears and lances that the Philistines had dropped. And not one enemy soldier dared turn around to face the Hebrews and fight. Whoever was not killed, fled for his life as fast as his legs would carry him.

When the Hebrews finally stopped their victorious pursuit, they were just below the village of Beth-car, in the flowering plains of Sharon. In great happiness they gathered again before Samuel. They were now between Mizpah and the village of Shen. Samuel found a huge boulder and set it down before him. "Let this stone be called *evven ha-ezer*," he told his people, *"the stone of help;* and let it be a reminder and a witness that until here Eternal Lord has helped us."

It was to be a long time before the Philistines felt courage enough to think of war against the Hebrews. Against men, no matter how strong, they could fight. But how could they stand up against an unseen Divine Ruler who sent earthquake and thunder and lightning at the very moment they were going to destroy the Hebrews in a crushing defeat? (And this same Divine Ruler had sent them those dreadful plagues.)

When the five Philistine rulers wondered why the God of Israel was defending His people now, their priests and seers know the answer: Israel had a new leader named Samuel, who made his people throw out their idols.

So it was that as long as Samuel remained alive and strong, the Philistines stayed in their own fortified cities and villages, daring to make no war against Israel. In all the land that the Philistines had captured over the many years, the Hebrews now came back; in every captive town and village they lived freely and happily once more.

The land of Israel knew it had an excellent leader. Wherever he went, Samuel found that the people revered

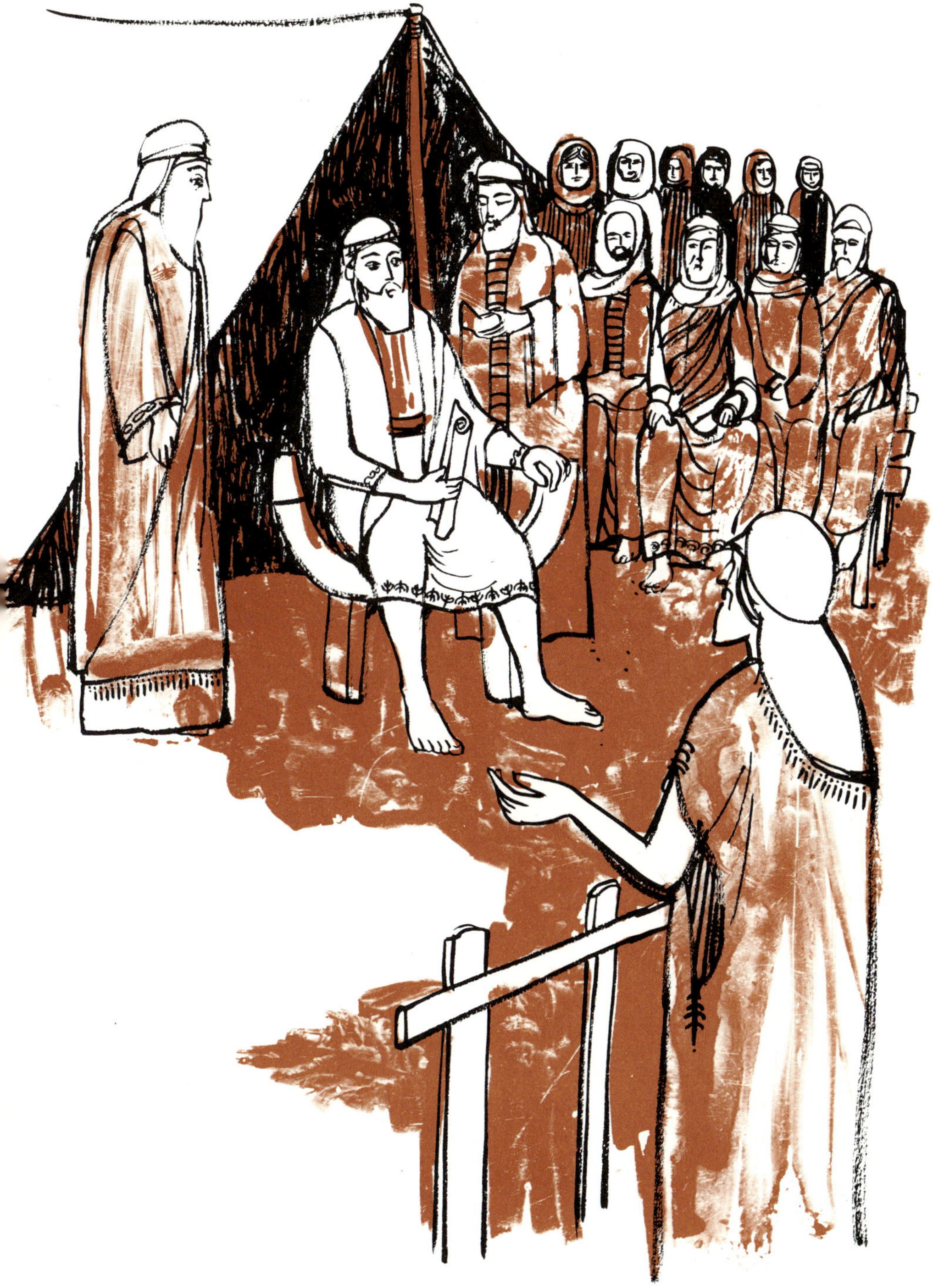

him and listened to him. For now they knew, beyond any possible doubt, that he was a man of God.

Samuel continued to live in the manner he had chosen. Every year without fail he set out from his home in Ramah to travel his circuit through the villages and towns of Israel. From Ramah he made his way to Bethel, then on to Gilgal, and then to Mizpah. In each of these places there was an altar, where the people could gather to bring offerings to the Almighty. And at each of these places Samuel sat as a judge, to listen to quarrels, arguments and complaints among the people that they wanted him to settle.

And always Samuel took with him a tent and a plentiful supply of food and provisions, so that he took nothing whatsoever from anyone—no payments and no gifts. For enough grew on his family's farm in Ramah to give him everything he needed.

There was one more thing that Samuel always took with him: a scroll of the Torah. At every stopping-place he taught it and explained it to the people—a bit at a time—so that they might know what the Almighty wanted of them. And the people listened, and obeyed.

Having ended his round of his travels, Samuel returned to Ramah—until a new year came, making it time for him to set out again. Many who could not see him during his travels would visit him then in Ramah, to receive his wise advice and his blessing.

In Ramah, too, Samuel married; and his wife bore him two sons. As he watched his sons growing to manhood with the passing years, Samuel felt grateful and deeply happy that he had become a true servant of the Almighty. He was blessed to be able to bring his people serenity and peace under the Almighty's protection.

And the Hebrews were thankful and happy with him, knowing that not since Moses and Aaron had there been so great a prophet and leader in Israel.